PIPE FITTINGS

 NIPPLES

 PIPE LENGTHS UP TO 22 FT.

 STRAIGHT COUPLING

 REDUCING COUPLING

 COUPLING

 NUT

 CAP

 STRAIGHT TEE

 REDUCING TEE

 STREET TEE

 STRAIGHT CROSS

REDUCING CROSS

 90° ELBOW

90° ELBOW

90° ELBOW · 45° ELBOW · REDUCING ELBOW · 90° STREET ELBOW · 45° STREET ELBOW · 45° Y-BEND

 REDUCING TEE

REDUCER

 UNION (3 PARTS) · PLUG · BUSHING · CAP · RETURN BEND

 90° · 45° · STREET — UNION ELBOWS · UNION TEES

 PLUG · 45° ELBOW · TEE

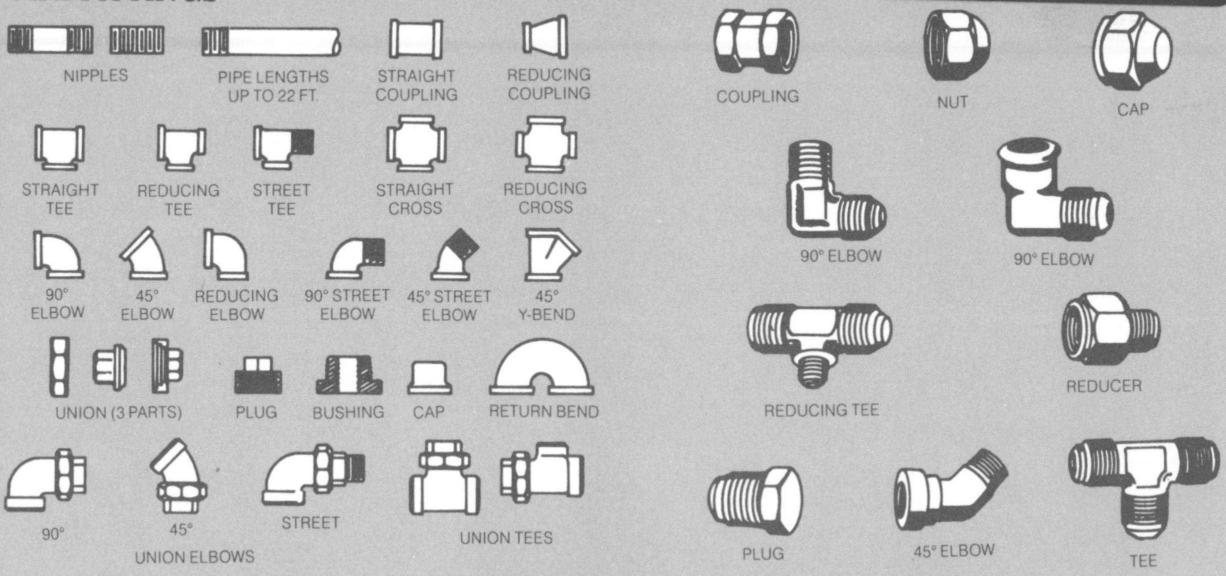

MEASURES OF CAPACITY

1 cup	=	8 fl oz
2 cups	=	1 pint
2 pints	=	1 quart
4 quarts	=	1 gallon
2 gallons	=	1 peck
4 pecks	=	1 bushel

STANDARD STEEL PIPE ((All Dimensions in inches)

Nominal Size	Outside Diameter	Inside Diameter	Nominal Size	Outside Diameter	Inside Diameter
⅛	0.405	0.269	1	1.315	1.049
¼	0.540	0.364	1¼	1.660	1.380
⅜	0.675	0.493	1½	1.900	1.610
½	0.840	0.622	2	2.375	2.067
¾	1.050	0.824	2½	2.875	2.469

WOOD SCREWS

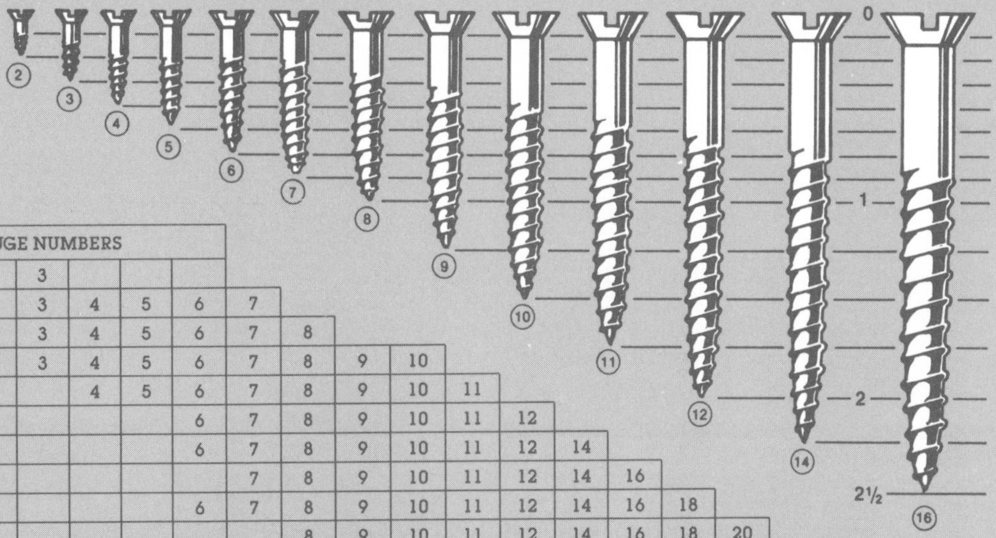

LENGTH	GAUGE NUMBERS													
¼ INCH	0	1	2	3										
⅜ INCH			2	3	4	5	6	7						
½ INCH			2	3	4	5	6	7	8					
⅝ INCH				3	4	5	6	7	8	9	10			
¾ INCH					4	5	6	7	8	9	10	11		
⅞ INCH							6	7	8	9	10	11	12	
1 INCH							6	7	8	9	10	11	12	14
1¼ INCH								7	8	9	10	11	12	14	16
1½ INCH							6	7	8	9	10	11	12	14	16	18
1¾ INCH									8	9	10	11	12	14	16	18	20
2 INCH									8	9	10	11	12	14	16	18	20
2¼ INCH										9	10	11	12	14	16	18	20
2½ INCH													12	14	16	18	20
2¾ INCH														14	16	18	20
3 INCH															16	18	20
3½ INCH																18	20	24
4 INCH																18	20	24

WHEN YOU BUY SCREWS, SPECIFY (1) LENGTH, (2) GAUGE NUMBER, (3) TYPE OF HEAD—FLAT, ROUND, OR OVAL, (4) MATERIAL— STEEL, BRASS, BRONZE, ETC., (5) FINISH—BRIGHT, STEEL BLUED, CADMIUM, NICKEL, OR CHROMIUM PLATED.

Popular Mechanics

do-it-yourself encyclopedia

The complete, illustrated home reference guide from the world's most authoritative source for today's how-to-do-it information.

Volume 21

SANDERS

to

SHOP PROJECTS

HEARST DIRECT BOOKS

NEW YORK

Acknowledgements

The Popular Mechanics Encyclopedia is published with the consent and cooperation of POPULAR MECHANICS Magazine.

For POPULAR MECHANICS Magazine:

Editor-in-Chief: *Joe Oldham*
Managing Editor: *Bill Hartford*
Special Features Editor: *Sheldon M. Gallager*
Automotive Editor: *Wade A. Hoyt, SAE*
Home and Shop Editor: *Steve Willson*
Electronics Editor: *Stephen A. Booth*
Boating, Outdoors and Travel Editor: *Timothy H. Cole*
Science Editor: *Dennis Eskow*

Popular Mechanics Encyclopedia

Project Director: *Boyd Griffin*
Manufacturing: *Ron Schoenfeld*
Assistant Editors: *Cynthia W. Lockhart, Peter McCann, Rosanna Petruccio*
Production Coordinator: *Peter McCann*

The staff of Popular Mechanics Encyclopedia is grateful to the following individuals and organizations:
Editor: *C. Edward Cavert*
Editor Emeritus: *Clifford B. Hicks*
Production: *Layla Productions*
Production Director: *Lori Stein*
Book Design: *The Bentwood Studio*
Art Director: *Jos. Trautwein*
Design Consultant: *Suzanne Bennett & Associates*
Illustrations: *AP Graphics, Evelyne Johnson Associates, Popular Mechanics Magazine, Vantage Art.*

Contributing Writers: C.E. Banister, *Cutting board for your shop,* page 2655; R.C. Barnes, *Spool cabinet,* page 2619; Walter E. Burton, *Stand for your sander,* page 2576; *Tool holders from hardware cloth,* page 2654; *Drilling hard materials,* page 2663; *Drill angled holes accuratgely,* page 2665; Rosario Capotosto, *Butler's table you can build,* page 2585; *Lazy susan table server,* page 2603; Frank H. Day *Angle blocks for miter cuts,* page 2672; Jorma Hyypia, *Keep your shop organized,* page 2646; M.R. Kirstein, *Shop organizers,* page 2651; W. Clyde Lammey, *Sawhorse that's simple and easy,* page 2580; Wayne C. Leckey, *Folding snack server,* page 2588; *Electric serving cart,* page 2592; *Sewing center for every taste and need,* page 2605; Mike McClintock, *How to use shims,* page 2668; Burt Murphy, *Belt sander techniques,* page 2564; Joseph R. Provey, *Take the hazards out of your home shop,* page 2659; Fred W. Schuleter, *Sharpen twist drills,* page 2627; Bob Stearns, *Putting and edge on sportsman's tools,* page 2634; William G. Waggoner, *Sharpen tools on your radial-arm saw,* page 2625; *Jig to sharpen bandsaw blades,* page 2630; William G. Waggoner and John A. Haase, *Mitre boards,* page 2669; Kenneth Wells, *Oilstone can be self-lubricating,* page 2632; Harry Wicks, *Belt sanding basics,* page 2568; *Pad sander know-how,* page 2570; *Early American server,* page 2597; Craig Wilson, *Utility shelf coverup,* page 2642; Wyatt Yousay, *Eggs hold small parts,* page 2652.

ISBN 0-87851-174-1

Library of Congress 85-81760

10   9   8   7   6   5   4

PRINTED IN THE UNITED STATES OF AMERICA

Although every effort has been made to ensure the accuracy and completeness of the information in this book, Hearst Direct Books makes no guarantees, stated or implied, nor will they be liable in the event of misinterpretation or human error made by the reader, or for any typographical errors that may appear. WORK SAFELY WITH HAND TOOLS. WEAR SAFETY GOGGLES. READ MANUFACTURER'S INSTRUCTIONS AND WARNINGS FOR ALL PRODUCTS.

Contents

Belt sander techniques

■ THE BELT SANDER is a workhorse of a tool. Faced with a job that would be dirty and tedious by hand, a belt sander will literally chew its way through the chore effortlessly. Actually, once you own one, you'll wonder how you ever got along without it.

Using a belt sander, you will find that with a little practice you'll spend a lot less time on such tasks as:
- Sanding rough stock smooth.
- Removing old finish.
- Putting a bevel on a door.
- Reducing stock thickness.
- Back-cutting miter cuts for neater joints (casings, for example).
- Dressing up a poor saw cut.
- Polishing and buffing.

If you have never used a belt sander before, take the time to familiarize yourself with it when you first get one. Since a belt sander is larger, livelier and heavier than a pad sander or drill-disc combination, it does take some getting used to. Hefting, changing belts, adjusting belt tracking and the pull as the sanding belt digs into the workpiece will all be new to you. To gain this experience, use the tool on various materials: hard and soft woods, metals, plastic laminate and any others that you usually work with.

The belt sander should always be turned on before contact is made with the workpiece and turned off after it is lifted off. When lowering the sander to the material, you should keep the flat platen parallel to the work. Once it contacts the workpiece, keep the sander moving to prevent "dishing out." The weight of the sander itself provides adequate pressure; all you need do is guide the machine. Bearing down on the sander

LATEST DESIGN TREND by most makers lets you use power for flush sanding next to a vertical surface.

COARSE-GRIT BELT sands rough stock smooth in a few minutes. Finer-grit belts are used to finish the job.

TO WORK small pieces, sander can be clamped upside down on the workbench to free both of your hands.

EVENLY POLISHED FINISHES on metal are possible in the workshop using special belts and lubricant.

TO STRIP PAINT, use a coarse, open paper to start, then complete the job with a finer, closed-coat belt.

NYLON WEB BELT and small amount of cutting oil clean dirty-plywood surface and produce even tones.

can, in fact, cause damage. When working with wood, move the sander with the grain of the wood, never across. Work the entire surface, overlapping each succeeding pass. If you attempt to complete a 3-in. strip and then move over for successive strips, you will end up with a wavy surface.

The sanders shown on these pages are all basically the same, with slight design variations. Most manufacturers offer at least one model equipped with a dust collector. It's a good feature and it adds little to the total cost. If you do a lot of sanding, or if your family hasn't been too happy with the dust settling in the laundry room, the

CONCRETE FLOOR STAINS can be cleaned with a belt sander. The tool's not limited to wood and metal.

LUMPY CONCRETE on basement window sill is removed using coarse grit. Here a dust collector pays off.

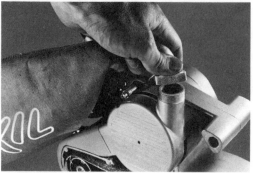

DUST COLLECTOR on this sander is a tube and bag connected to the unit with a threaded, knurled ring.

A SPRING-TENSIONED slip-in nozzle is connected to the bag on this model.

HOSE AND NOZZLE serve as dust collector on this sander—they're attached to vacuum cleaner.

CLAMPED ON ITS SIDE, the belt sander can be used for "planing" jobs. Vertical board serves as a fence.

extra couple of dollars that a collector costs will be money well spent.

In addition to on-the-job uses, a sander can also be rigged with clamps for use as a bench-type power sander. Small-size workpieces can then be brought to the sander and, since you are saved the task of hefting the tool, both hands are free to guide the work against the belt.

Both general and special-purpose abrasive papers are manufactured for use with belt sanders. Aluminum oxide, manufactured in a wide variety of grits, is the type you will use most often. Or, you can use special-purpose belts to convert the belt sander for use as a cleaner, buffer and polisher for metals, woods, plastics and laminates.

Belt sanding facts you should know:
- *Wood finishing.* For final finishing of furniture

HELD IN ONE SPOT too long, a belt sander will plow a deep groove (shown across the grain here).

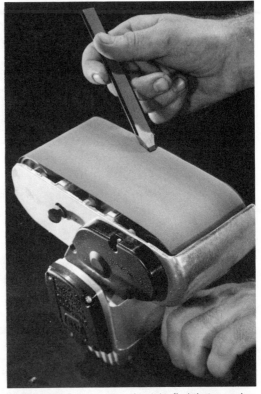

CARPENTERS on construction jobs find that a sander offers a fast way to sharpen a pencil to a keen point.

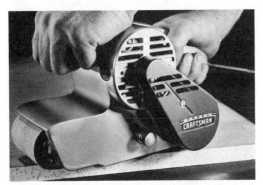

USING AN 80-GRIT BELT, plastic laminate self-edge is quickly and easily smoothed flush with plywood.

WORKBENCH STAND comes with accurate miter gauge, secures the sander.

or cabinetry, use as many progressively finer grits as possible. The object here is to remove any marks left by the coarser belt that preceded the one being used.

• *Metal finishing.* Beeswax or tallow are recommended for use as lubricants for metal sanding, polishing or stain finishing. Several man-ufacturers market commercial lubricants for metal sanding.

• *Refinishing.* When removing paint, varnish or lacquer, use a coarse grade, open-coat belt for the initial stripping. Then change to closed-coat belts as the material shows through the coating. Use short, light strokes to avoid burning the coating and for longer belt life.

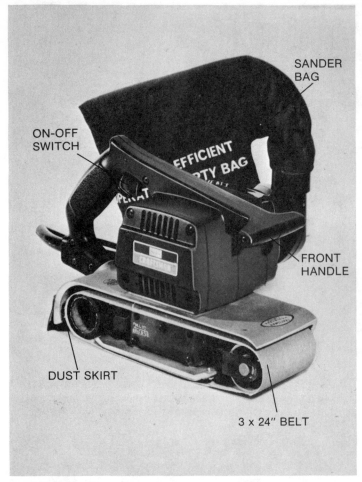

ON-OFF
SWITCH

SANDER
BAG

FRONT
HANDLE

DUST SKIRT

3 x 24″ BELT

BELT SANDER SIZE (i.e. 3x24 in., above) refers to
the width and length of belt that the tool uses. Size of
sander shown is suited for most jobs.

Belt sanding basics

■ THE PORTABLE belt sander is one of the favored homeowner power tools. Surprisingly, though, many people who own the tool do not know how to get the most out of it. And that is a pity, because a belt sander can save literally hours of hard work, and provide a smoother finish than most of us have the patience to achieve when rubbing by hand.

Though available in a great variety of configurations and sizes, all belt sanders work on the same principle—a loop or belt of adhesive grit travels in a straight line around two drums and across a platen. Platen size is important because this is the actual area of the belt that is sanding when the belt is traveling. Because of the belt sander's power, it is very important that you use the tool correctly:

● Always keep the platen flat on the work or you will create gouges, bevels and the like.

● Always keep the sander moving. The test run across the grain (see photo) gives a dramatic example of what results when a belt sander is left running too long in one spot.

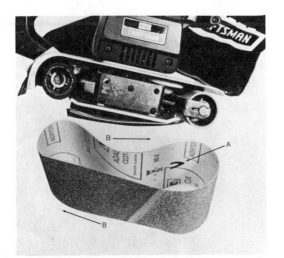

BELTS ARE MARKED for correct installation. Arrow A on the belt should always travel in the direction shown by arrows B or it may rip on the seam.

SMALL STOP—thinner than workpiece—is a must. It frees both hands for managing tool.

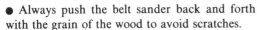

AFTER YOU RELIEVE drum tension according to the instructions, the belt simply slips on.

TEST RUN shows power of a belt sander and why you should keep it moving on the work.

ON THIS MODEL, the tension is created when the small latch is released (bottom photo).

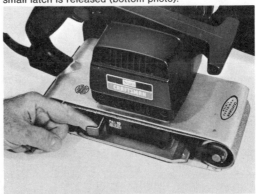

● Always push the belt sander back and forth with the grain of the wood to avoid scratches.

● Always make sure that you have adequate electrical cord to reach the full length of the work. If you forget to check this out beforehand, you stand a good chance of the line stopping the sander in midstroke—with inevitable gouging of work. If you should require an extension cord, make certain that you use the right wire size—not a lamp cord.

When you buy a belt sander, your dealer probably will stock the most popular homeowner sizes—3x21 in. and 3x24 in.—as well as some larger professional models. You are well advised to pick one of the homeowner sizes. Greater size also means greater weight you must heft around.

Pad sander know-how

■ NO MATTER WHAT other uses you have for your pad sander—some people have been known to use the felt pad for massages—this power tool is designed basically to make finishing easier. That's why it's popularly called a finishing sander.

Make no mistake about it, a pad sander is a great saver of time and effort. A project that might take hours if sanded by hand can be done in a fraction of that time with power.

Besides saving time, a power pad sander lets you do a better job. There is no way you can smooth a flat surface by hand as efficiently as you can with abrasive paper clamped about the felt pad of a sander.

Though a finishing sander is one of the first three power tools most do-it-yourselfers buy, it is often a misused tool. It is not uncommon for a beginner (and even experienced woodworkers) to use the pad sander for jobs that would be best

performed by other tools such as the block plane or belt sander. In any event, remember that the tool is not designed for heavy stock removal.

Basically, the pad sander is used to finish-sand wood just prior to applying the stain and finish to a project. By changing paper (grits), the tool also can be used to smooth paints, varnishes, lac-

PAPERS SIZED to suit various makers' sander shoes come packaged in all-one-grit or with mixed grits.

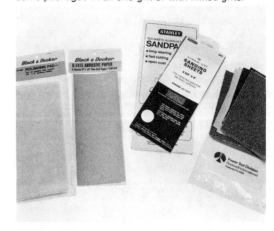

AUXILIARY HANDLE

ON-OFF SWITCH

LINE CORD

HANDLE

SANDING PLATE

PAD

ON-OFF SWITCH

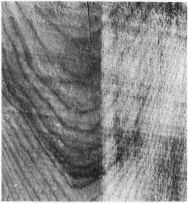

DIFFERENT MANUFACTURERS use various kinds of on-off switches. Model shown above has a thumb-operated slide type (inset) instead of toggle switch. A two-way sander (top right) gives you a choice between straight-line (center photo) and orbital sanding (bottom photo).

quers and the like between coats. Finally, when fitted with a lamb's-wool pad, a pad sander can be used with polishes and paste waxes to bring furniture to a high luster.

WEAR SAFETY GOGGLES

Types of pad sanders

There are two types, straight-line and orbital. The former has a back-and-forth motion which makes it ideal for with-the-grain sanding as you get close to the final stages of the sanding opera-

SANDPAPER COMES in a wide variety of grits, from left—wet or dry fine, 280, 120, 100, 80 and 60.

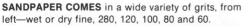

METHOD OF HOLDING sandpaper varies with makers. This model uses a lever release.

TYPICAL PAD-SANDER CHORES

TO SAND corner with minimum chatter, let side of shoe (not end) contact vertical.

NARROW SURFACE can be accurately sanded if you work carefully.

PAD SANDER gets into tight corners; the orbital type usually leaves marks here.

SAND SMALL objects by clamping sander upside down. Don't overtighten the clamp.

FITTED WITH a polishing pad, sander brings paste wax to a smooth, high luster.

WITH CARE and fine emery paper, in a pinch, sander can hone a chisel.

tion. The straight-line action removes stock more slowly than the orbital type, but does a smoother job. On some soft woods, stock removal can be speeded up by sanding across the grain in the early coarse-grit stages.

Orbital sanders, on the other hand, combine a slight side-to-side motion with a back-and-forth motion to form small orbits. If speed is slow, swirls will be obvious on the finished product and mar its beauty.

Both types are readily available, and now most manufacturers offer sander models which combine both actions in one tool.

Choosing a pad sander

The pad sander is a simple tool—one which you can learn to use correctly in a short time. Before buying one, the smartest thing you can do is to pick up and heft the various models you are considering. The better hardware and building supply outlets usually have sample boards available for customer tool tests.

By using this service, you will quickly find out that some tools feel extra comfortable in your hand, while others will be just plain cumbersome. Now is the time—before spending—to find out whether or not a tool gives you satisfactory working comfort.

You will also have to decide whether you want straight-line or orbital action or both. Many craftsmen are content with an orbital sander with a high speed and very small orbits. With one of these, it is just about impossible to see any swirl marks in the finished project unless you have super vision (or use a magnifying glass). These models also cost more than their slower, larger-orbiting cousins.

Of course, with coarse-grit paper, almost any orbital sander is certain to produce some swirl marks. A 40-grit paper was used on a piece of birch to demonstrate the look of sander swirls in the photo.

If you opt for a dual-action model, make certain that the switch controlling the sander action is easy to use, yet located and operated in such a way as to avoid accidental changing of sanding strokes.

As with all power tools, you get what you pay for in pad sanders. In general, it's safe to say that the higher the price, the better the quality will be: The construction of the tool plus the number and type of bearings definitely affect the sander's price tag.

As a rule of thumb, you can figure that the most inexpensive sanders will serve just fine for the once-in-a-while user. Those equipping a woodworking shop, with the idea of doing most home handyman chores themselves and taking on occasional furniture projects, will usually be content with a tool in the middle price range.

In general, the highest priced pad sanders are geared for the professional market. However, many serious do-it-yourselfers want the best tools; for these, sanders rated commercial or industrial are the only choices.

Mounting paper

There are as many different ways of putting sandpaper in a pad sander as there are pad sanders. Some tools are easy to load and some are not. Check this feature before buying and pick a sander that makes it easy to mount and remove papers.

No matter how paper is mounted and held, it must remain flat as well as secure. The action of the sander itself is a pulling one, and if the paper is loose and flaps about, it will soon tear and become useless.

Check the maker's instructions for mounting papers and make certain that all papers you mount are stretched tightly across the pad.

The shoe (or pad) on most sanders is sized so you will be able to get three strips of paper from a standard-size sheet of abrasive paper. Some of the commercial-duty sanders have larger shoes; with these you get two sander-size pieces from each sheet. Sized sandpapers are also available as accessories: These are packaged both in assorted grits and in all-one-type papers.

Maintaining the sander

No matter what price tool you buy, it will last longer if you use and maintain it properly. Pad sander maintenance, for the most part, consists of little more than keeping the air ports free of dust accumulation (so the tool won't overheat) and periodic lubrication. The best way to do the former is by blowing out the tool with compressed air. If you lack a compressor, periodically take your sander to the local gas station to blow out all dust. If you do own a compressor, use it on the sander after every work session. Lubricate the tool following the manufacturer's instructions with regard to points, frequency and type of lubricant to use. Today, many sanders are sealed and require no further lubrication by the owner. But since that's not the case for all sanders, carefully read that section of the manual covering lubrication.

Using the tool

No matter which type of pad sander you buy, it will come equipped with a felt pad on its shoe. The rigidity—or degree of softness—of this pad is intended to suit most of the average jobs a do-it-yourselfer encounters. However, on occasion a softer or harder pad is required.

For example, on some plastics, woods with hard-and-soft grains and for honing of chisels, a more-rigid pad is desirable. In this event, you simply place a piece of ⅛-in. hardboard between the paper and felt pad. To hold it in place, drive three or four brads through the hardboard and into the felt.

If the occasion demands a softer pad, try substituting foam rubber for the felt pad.

Some sanders come equipped with an auxiliary handle. On certain jobs, such as for vertical sanding, this can be very handy. A spare handle is often useful on the bench, too, because two-hand operation will assist you in keeping the shoe flat on the workpiece.

No matter which action your sander has—orbital or straight-line—it is usually best to work the tool back and forth parallel with the grain of the wood.

When edge sanding a narrow surface, use both hands to maintain maximum control. If the job is a critical one, clamp boards on both sides of the surface being sanded to prevent any chance of rounding over corners.

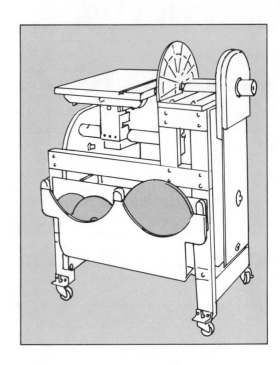

Disc and drum sander you can build

■ BESIDES BEING an excellent disc and drum sander, this inexpensive tool can perform other functions, such as buffing, wire brushing, deburring and light grinding. The adjustable table can be removed for buffing large objects.

If you desire, the mandrel speed can be varied by using a two-step pulley on the motor. Operate a 12-in. sanding disc at about 1725 rpm, an 8-in. disc as high as 3450 rpm for the most efficient work.

Start by making and assembling the end members. Install the mandrel support with lagscrews and the way supports with carriage bolts. Make the ways from 1¾-in.-dia. round stock (or the largest available to you) and bore holes in J and K to suit. Slots, cut 1½ in. deep in ends of ways, allow easy insertion.

The table is clamped to the ways with pieces B. These are made by clamping two pieces together and boring for the ways or by boring holes in a 3½ x 3½-in. block first, then resawing to suit on a bandsaw. Plane about ¹⁄₁₆ in. off the inside faces of B after boring to ensure good clamping action. Tilt table is controlled by a miter-gauge head available from many tool dealers.

The mandrel unit must be carefully mounted so it's perpendicular to the miter slot in the table. The ½-hp, 3450-rpm motor is mounted to a piece of ¾-in. plywood, which, in turn, is attached to the motor shelf with a standard 3½-in. door hinge.

CUSTOM STAND boasts a guard for the belt and pulley, and a tilting table.

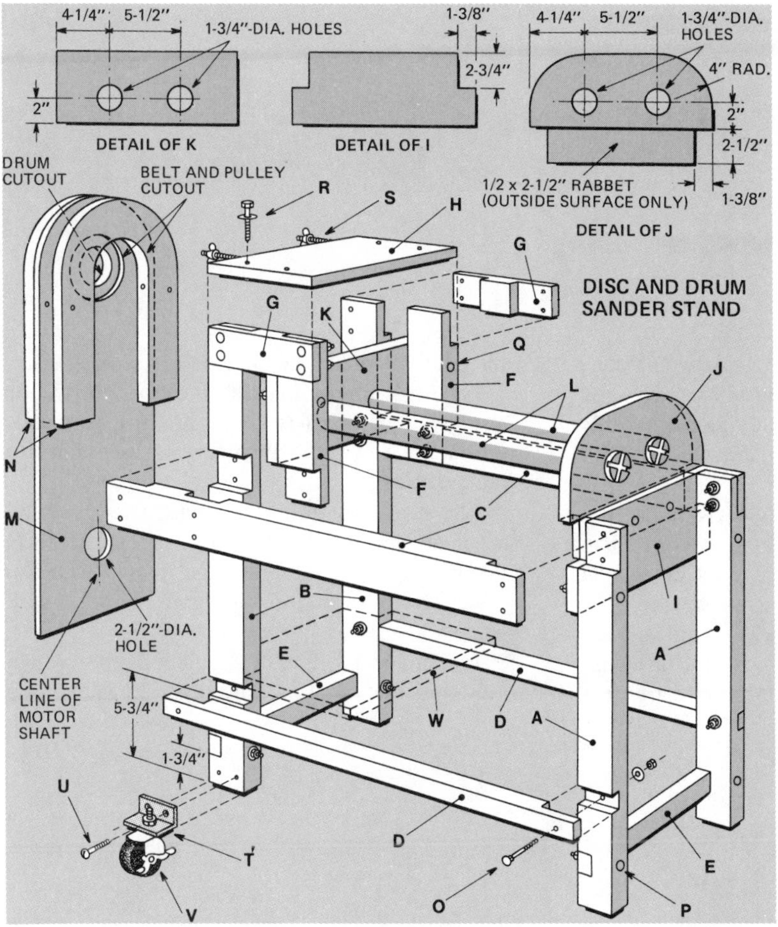
4-1/4"
5-1/2"
1-3/4"-DIA. HOLES
2"
DETAIL OF K
1-3/8"
2-3/4"
DETAIL OF I
4-1/4"
5-1/2"
1-3/4"-DIA. HOLES
4" RAD.
2"
2-1/2"
1/2 x 2-1/2" RABBET (OUTSIDE SURFACE ONLY)
1-3/8"
DETAIL OF J
DRUM CUTOUT
BELT AND PULLEY CUTOUT
DISC AND DRUM SANDER STAND
2-1/2"-DIA. HOLE
CENTER LINE OF MOTOR SHAFT
5-3/4"
1-3/4"
A
B
C
D
E
F
G
H
I
J
K
L
M
N
O
P
Q
R
S
T
U
V
W

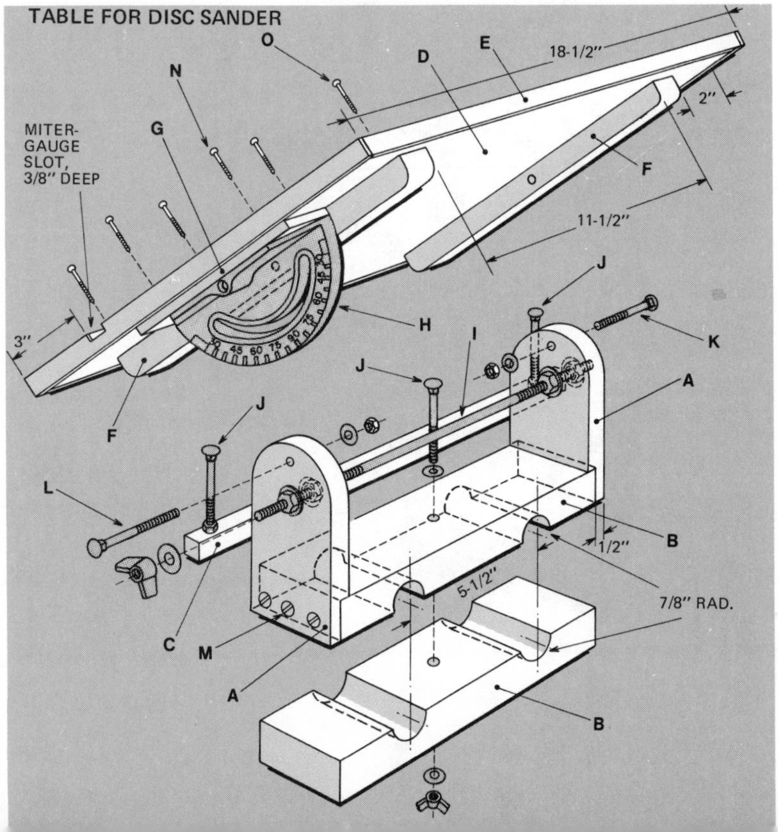
TABLE FOR DISC SANDER
MITER-GAUGE SLOT, 3/8" DEEP
18-1/2"
2"
11-1/2"
3"
1/2"
5-1/2"
7/8" RAD.
A
B
C
D
E
F
G
H
I
J
K
L
M
N
O

MATERIALS LIST—SANDER STAND

Key	No.	Size and description (use)
A	2	1⅜ x 2⅝ x 21" oak or fir (leg)
B	2	1⅜ x 2⅝ x 29⅜" oak or fir (leg)*
C	2	1⅜ x 2¾ x 28" oak or fir (rail)*
D	2	1⅜ x 1¼ x 28" oak or fir (side rail)*
E	2	1⅜ x 1¼ x 14" oak or fir (end rail)*
F	2	1⅜ x 2⅝ x 11" oak or fir*
G	2	1⅜ x 2⅝ x 7" oak or fir*
H	1	¾ x 7 x 14" oak or fir*
I	1	1⅛ x 5½ x 14" oak, fir or pine
J	1	1⅛ x 8¼ x 14" oak, fir or pine
K	1	1⅛ x 5½ x 14" oak, fir or pine
L	2	1¾"-dia. x 24" round stock (ways)
M	1	¼ x 8¾ x 29½" birch plywood*
N	1	¾ x 8¾ x 14" birch plywood (guard)*
O	24	¼ x 1¾" carriage bolts, washers, nuts
P	4	¼ x 3" carriage bolts, washers, nuts
Q	2	¼ x 4" carriage bolts, washers, nuts
R	4	¼ x 2" lagscrews
S	2	¼ x 4" hanger bolts, wingnuts (guard fastener)
T	4	3/16 x 1¼ x 1¼ x 2⅝" angle iron
U	8	¼ x 2" fh stovebolts
V	4	2" locking casters
W	1	¾ x 14 x 14" plywood (shelf for motor)

MATERIALS LIST—SANDER TABLE

Key	No.	Size and description (use)
A	2	⅞ x 3⅜ x 6" oak, fir or pine*
B	2	1½ x 3⅜ x 10½" oak, fir or pine*
C	1	1 x 1 x 15" oak (leveler, nail to carriage)*
D	1	1 x 15½ x 18½" birch plywood [glue ¼" to ¾" piece]
E	4	¼ x 1" x length to suit birch edging
F	2	1½ x 1½ x 14" oak or fir
G	1	½ x 1¾ x 6½" oak or fir (spacer)
H	1	Cast-iron or oak miter head
I	1	⅜"-dia. x 12½" steel rod
J	3	¼"-dia. x 3½" carriage bolt, nuts, washers
K	1	¼"-dia. x 3" carriage bolt, nut, washer
L	1	¼ x 4½" carriage bolt, nut, washer
M	6	No. 8 x 2½" fh screws
N	2	No. 7 x 1¼" fh screws
O	8	No. 8 x 2" fh screws

* These are overall dimensions; pieces must be cut to fit.

MATERIALS LIST—DISC STORAGE

Key	No.	Size and description (use)
A	4	1 x 1½" x length to suit (space blocks)
B	1	¼" plywood, cut to suit

Misc.: White glue, ¾" brads as required.

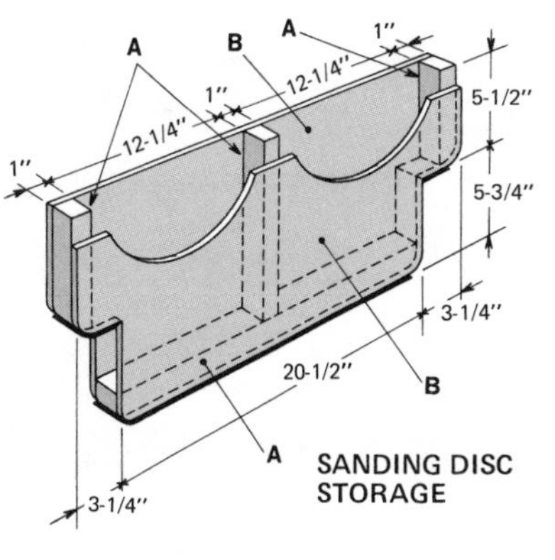
A
B
A
1"
12-1/4"
1"
12-1/4"
1"
5-1/2"
5-3/4"
3-1/4"
20-1/2"
B
A
3-1/4"
SANDING DISC STORAGE

Stand for your sander

■ EVER TRY TO SAND a 1-in. wood cube with a portable finishing sander? If you have, you probably wished you had the sander firmly anchored so you could manipulate the cube instead of the machine.

The wood stand shown here provides a firm mounting for a finishing sander and a convenient means of guiding small pieces, such as model parts, against its vibrating abrasive surface. The stand was designed to fit a Rockwell sander; other makes of machines can be used, of course, although the arrangement of the mounting blocks

and other elements might require some altering.

The work-supporting table is of ½-in. plywood; almost all other parts are from ¾-in. plywood. Ordinary ¾-in. pine lumber was used for the table column.

The sander platform was constructed first and mounted on the base with its outer longitudinal margin 1 in. from the base edge. The two vertical pieces were attached to the horizontal panel with glue and nails.

It is important that air circulate freely through the sander motor to prevent overheating. To

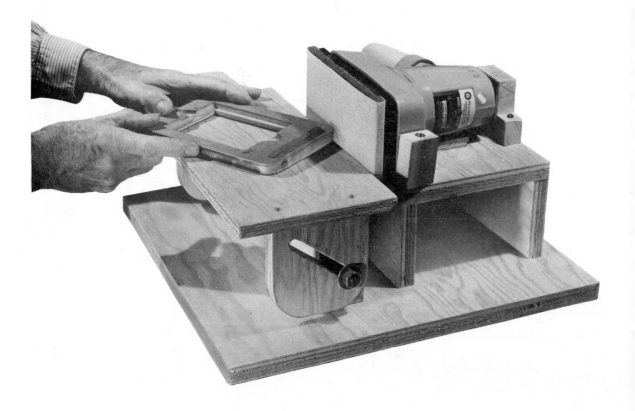

avoid any interference with air discharge from the vent openings nearer the platform when the sander is resting on its side, an opening was cut in the platform opposite these vents.

Three devices hold the sander firmly in position on its platform:

• A 1¼ x 8-in. strip of aluminum-siding sheet that projects ¼ in. above the platform surface, along the edge next to the work-supporting table. A leather strip, 1/16-in. thick, was glued to the side of this strip toward the platform. This acts as a cushion to prevent marring the sander housing. This padded strip projects into the space between the sander-housing edge and the sander pad, and prevents the sander from moving toward the work table.

• Leather-faced wooden blocks installed to hold the sander against the leather-padded aluminum strip. Two of these blocks flank the housing near the sanding pad, the third presses against the outer tip of the motor portion. Two more blocks are under the sander. One supports the motor housing, the other supports the handle.

• A leather strap, attached to the platform with

HOLD-DOWNS go on sander platform (top). At the right, the platform's blocks and strap are in place. Note the opening for air flow from the motor.

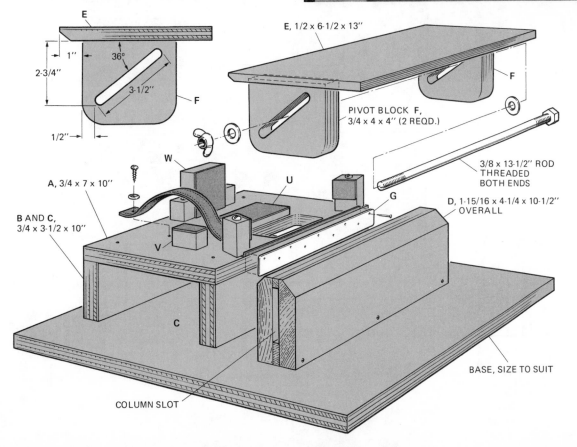

wood screws, and encircling the handle near the motor. Its purpose is to hold the sander in close contact with the two leather-faced blocks underneath. This strap should not be drawn too tight—just enough to keep the sander from moving upward. (For some sanders, it might be preferable to install the strap around the motor portion.) One end of the strap is anchored with two wood screws and washers, the other end by a single No. 8 wood screw installed after the sander is in position.

When a sander has to be removed and replaced frequently, a bolt-and-nut arrangement might be preferable.

The two blocks flanking the housing near the sander pad are secured with single, No. 12 flathead screws 3 in. long, permitting the blocks to adjust to the angle of the housing surface. The block supporting the motor housing was nailed to the platform before leather was applied, and the handle block was similarly fastened with a flathead wood screw. Two No. 8 screws hold the third block.

When the sander is running, there is some vibration transmitted to the platform. No tests were made to determine the long-range durability of the anchoring system, but no tendencies for the blocks to loosen, or other restraints to lessen, were noted.

The workpiece is normally rested on an adjustable table made from ½-in. plywood. Projecting downward from the table are two "pivot blocks," each having a diagonal slot. These blocks straddle the ends of a table column in which there is a vertical slot that measures about $\frac{7}{16}$ in. wide and 2¾ in. high. This slot was created by assembling the column from two ¾-in. pieces separated by a $\frac{7}{16}$-in.-sq. and a $\frac{7}{16}$ x 1-in. spacing strip. The column was mounted with the vertical centerline of its slot about 1¾ in. from the abrasive surface.

Length of the table-supporting column is ½ in. greater than the length of the sander platform. This provides clearance for the slotted pivot blocks to overlap the platform when the table is adjusted to a steep angle. Pivot blocks are positioned on the table so the distance between them matches the column length.

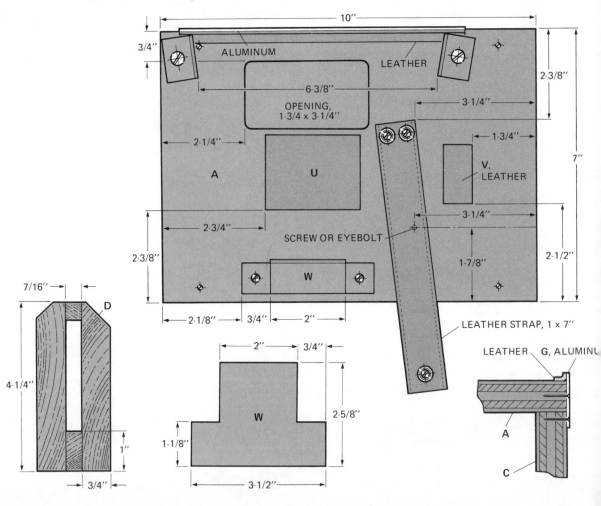

The combination of diagonal slots in the pivot blocks and vertical slot in the column provides for an infinite number of settings for the table with respect to angle and vertical adjustment, and total vertical movement is nearly 2 in.

A ⅜-in. rod, 13½ in. long, threaded at both ends, runs through pivot-block and column slots. It has a wingnut on one end and an ordinary nut on the other plus two washers. Tightening the wingnut compresses the pivot blocks against the column ends, securely anchoring the table.

You may have to trim the column top by trial and error so the table can be tilted up to 45° without moving the table edge too far from the abrasive edge.

Although the sanding stand could be used without anchoring it to the bench, it does have some tendency to "walk." Use either a ¾-in. sponge rubber pad between base and bench or C-clamps to eliminate "walking."

PROTOTYPE stand was tailored to Rockwell's Model 65 sander. Alter dimensions as needed for others.

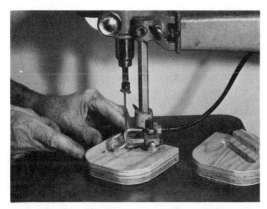

CUT PIVOT block slot by drilling holes at the ends, connecting them with jig or coping saw.

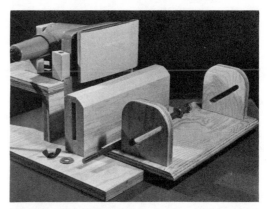

SUPPORT COLUMN is ready to receive pivot blocks for the work-support table at the right.

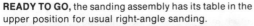

READY TO GO, the sanding assembly has its table in the upper position for usual right-angle sanding.

PIVOT-BLOCK and support-column slots combine to let the work table take virtually any angle.

Sawhorse that's simple and easy

■ IT TAKES DOWN and sets up in seconds. The legs fold flat in pairs, so you can stand them in a corner where shop space is limited. Or you can toss them into a pickup or the car trunk with room to spare. Set up, these horses will take heavy loads, shoves, knocks and poundings.

The beam is straight-grained hardwood—oak or maple is best—and ¾-in. oak should be used for the legs, or trestles. These are made in pairs, and care must be taken to make quite precise duplicates. Two legs are hinged together as indi-cated and the beam is dadoed at both ends, each dado being made at an angle of about 7 degrees. When making the dadoes, cut them with square, true shoulders and just a hair's breadth wider than the thickness of the leg stock. And be sure to cut a uniform depth of ¼ in.

After you have shaped the legs, clamp them in place in the dadoes and screw the strap hinge to each so that the pin just touches the lower edge of the beam. Then make the spreader as indi-cated from flat steel—sometimes referred to as band iron—and screw it to one leg. Then, with the legs in place spread them, swing the spreader down into position and mark the location of the screw which slips into the slot at the free end of the spreader. The trick here is to position all the parts and then exert a little extra pressure so that when the spreader is locked in place the upper ends of the legs in the dadoes will grip the beam tightly. This will assure that when you pick up the horse or move it about, the trestles will stay solidly in place.

The length of the beam, the height of the tres-tles and the finish are your options. For rough work there need be no finish at all, but for use in a "show" workshop you can stain and varnish to whatever color suits your fancy.

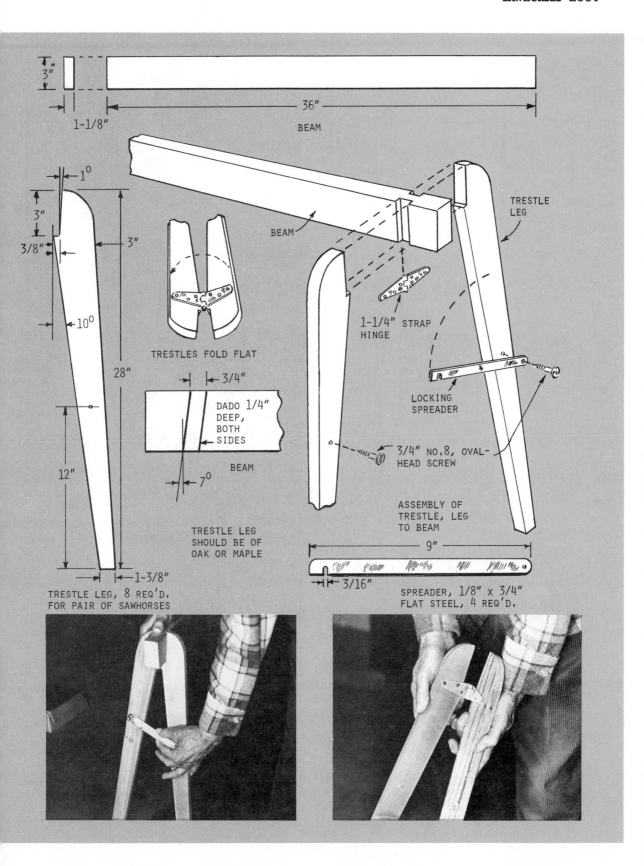

3"

1-1/8"

36"

BEAM

1°

3"

3/8"

3"

10°

28"

12"

1-3/8"

TRESTLE LEG, 8 REQ'D,
FOR PAIR OF SAWHORSES

BEAM

TRESTLES FOLD FLAT

3/4"

DADO 1/4"
DEEP,
BOTH
SIDES

BEAM

7°

TRESTLE LEG
SHOULD BE OF
OAK OR MAPLE

BEAM

TRESTLE
LEG

1-1/4" STRAP
HINGE

LOCKING
SPREADER

3/4" NO. 8, OVAL-
HEAD SCREW

ASSEMBLY OF
TRESTLE, LEG
TO BEAM

9"

3/16"

SPREADER, 1/8" x 3/4"
FLAT STEEL, 4 REQ'D.

Sawhorse becomes a workbench

■ A SAWHORSE need not be just a sawhorse; it can be the handiest home-repair "workbench" you ever saw. Fitted with a flat top, it provides a benchtop surface for all kinds of layout work, plus a place to clamp a vise.

When a shallow tray is fitted between the legs, you can keep your hand tools, nails and screws all in one handy place such as a toolbox.

When a piece of perforated hardboard is fastened to one side of the horse, you have a built-in tool panel on which to store countless small tools with clips.

And when you install a duplex receptacle in one of the sawhorse legs and wire it to a retractable power-cord reel, you have convenience plus when plugging in power tools.

To add such a receptacle, an outlet box is first installed in the leg in a cutout made to receive it. The female plug is cut off the end of the cord reel and the line is attached to the outlet box with a Romex connector. Finally, the receptacle is installed in the box, which is then fitted with a plate.

THE TOOL TRAY is permanently affixed—and adds rigidity—to the sawhorse legs. It offers a good storage area for portable tools, small parts, screws and nails.

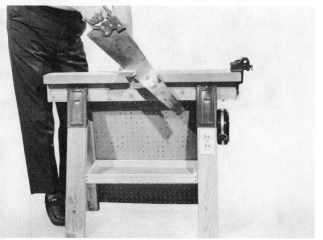

THE TOP WORK SURFACE is simply a bolted-on length of 2x6; ample for drilling, sawing and most other carpentry jobs.

AN ELECTRICAL OUTLET BOX is installed in one leg, with the line from a cord reel connected to the receptacle. The other end of the line is plugged into a power source.

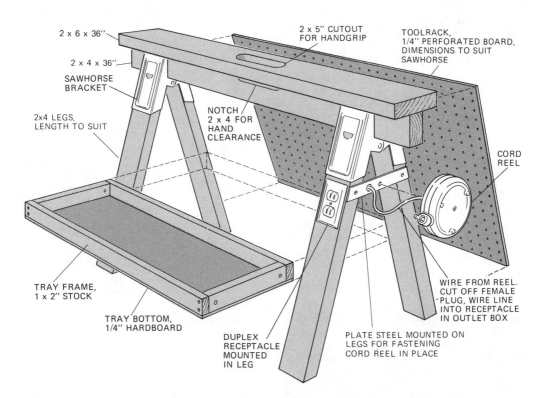

2 x 6 x 36''

2 x 4 x 36''

SAWHORSE BRACKET

2x4 LEGS, LENGTH TO SUIT

2 x 5'' CUTOUT FOR HANDGRIP

NOTCH 2 x 4 FOR HAND CLEARANCE

TOOLRACK, 1/4'' PERFORATED BOARD, DIMENSIONS TO SUIT SAWHORSE

CORD REEL

TRAY FRAME, 1 x 2'' STOCK

TRAY BOTTOM, 1/4'' HARDBOARD

DUPLEX RECEPTACLE MOUNTED IN LEG

PLATE STEEL MOUNTED ON LEGS FOR FASTENING CORD REEL IN PLACE

WIRE FROM REEL. CUT OFF FEMALE PLUG, WIRE LINE INTO RECEPTACLE IN OUTLET BOX

Sawbuck handles long logs

■ THIS SAWBUCK, with add-on support for safe, easy handling of long logs, makes cutting unwieldy logs a one-man job. The buck is assembled with carriage bolts and wingnuts to permit folding for against-the-wall storage. The extension, which is attached with a bolt that acts as a retaining pin, also folds flat.

Building the sawbuck is straight-forward. Cut pieces to the lengths given and cut angles and bevels as required. Then assemble with nails and bolts and waterproof glue as indicated. To attach the extension, glue block F, as shown in the drawing, to leg A and crosspiece E. Don't allow excess glue to seep into the X-joint. When the waterproof glue is thoroughly dry, drill the hole for the retaining pin.

MATERIALS LIST—SAWBUCK		
Key	No.	Size and description
A	4	1½ x 3½ x 48″ fir, trimmed to size
B	1	1½ x 3½ x 18″ fir
C	1	1½ x 3½ x 25½″ fir
D	1	1½ x 3½ x 52″ fir
E	4	¾ x 3½ x 22″ pine
F	1	1½ x 2 x 2″, cut from scrap 2 x 4
G	3	⅜ x 3½″ carriage bolts, washers and nuts
H	1	⅜ x 3½″ carriage bolt
I	8	6d common nails
J	1	4″ T-hinge

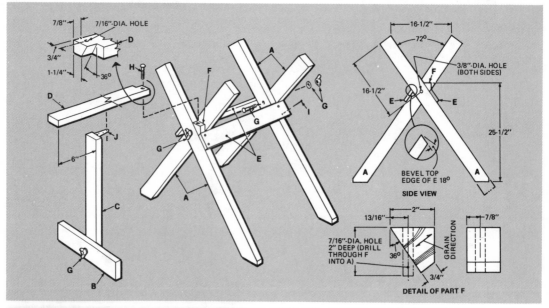

EXTENSION is notched to fit snugly into corner. Bolt serves as a retaining pin.

Butler's table you can build

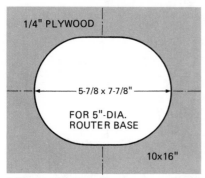

1/4" PLYWOOD

5-7/8 x 7-7/8"

FOR 5"-DIA.
ROUTER BASE

10x16"

A TEMPLATE forms mortises for both leaves of hinges in one quick router operation to save time.

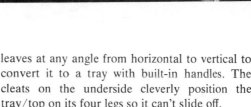

■ YOU'LL HAVE BOTH a coffee table and a serving tray when you make this attractive butler's table. When you have guests, its top lifts off for serving, then fits back firmly on the leg assembly when you use it as a table. As you can see, it is a beautiful table when you do careful work, and it is a handsome addition to any home.

The trick in making this project is to use friction hinges. These hinges let you position its four

leaves at any angle from horizontal to vertical to convert it to a tray with built-in handles. The cleats on the underside cleverly position the tray/top on its four legs so it can't slide off.

You can convert these plans to just about any size table. If you buy one like it in the store it will usually be 33x44 in. The one shown is made smaller than this.

Making this table and serving tray is not a

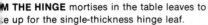

M THE HINGE mortises in the table leaves to .e up for the single-thickness hinge leaf.

USE A PLYWOOD TEMPLATE to guide the router base for cutting semicircular hinge mortises.

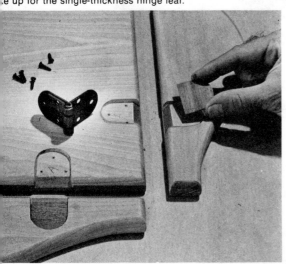

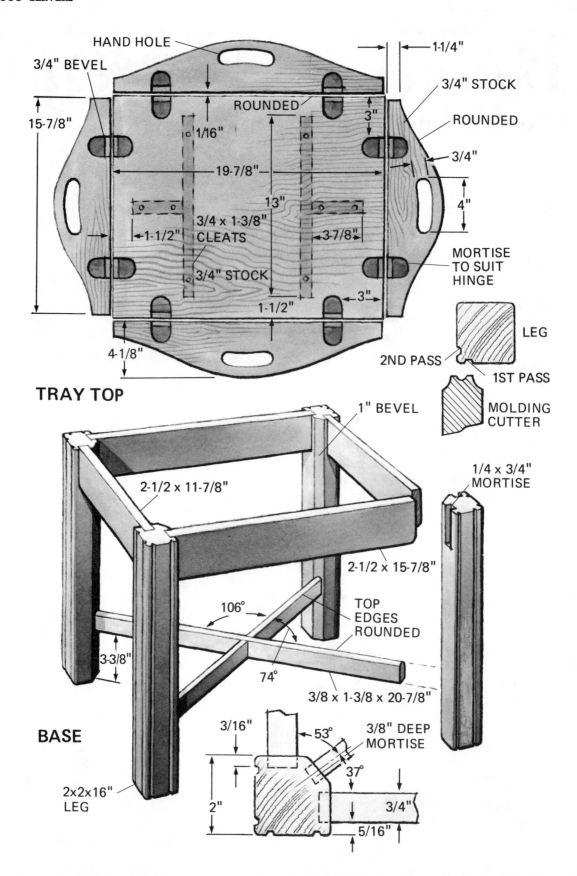

HAND HOLE

3/4" BEVEL

1-1/4"

3/4" STOCK

ROUNDED

ROUNDED

3"

3/4"

15-7/8"

1/16"

19-7/8"

13"

4"

3/4 x 1-3/8"
CLEATS

1-1/2"

3-7/8"

3/4" STOCK

MORTISE
TO SUIT
HINGE

1-1/2"

3"

4-1/8"

TRAY TOP

LEG

2ND PASS

1ST PASS

MOLDING
CUTTER

1" BEVEL

2-1/2 x 11-7/8"

1/4 x 3/4"
MORTISE

2-1/2 x 15-7/8"

106°

TOP
EDGES
ROUNDED

3-3/8"

74°

3/8 x 1-3/8 x 20-7/8"

BASE

3/16"

53°

3/8" DEEP
MORTISE

37°

3/4"

2x2x16"
LEG

2"

5/16"

difficult job, but neither is it a hammer-and-saw project. A router will form the semi-circular hinge mortises and round the edges. A table saw and molding cutter will form the decorative corner beading on the legs, a sabre saw will cut the tray leaves and hand grips and a drill press will form the stretcher mortises.

Make all legs alike

In the drawing, note that all four legs are made alike; the inner corners are first beveled 45°, then mortised at the top for the aprons and 3 in. up from the bottom for the stretchers. Use your table saw to rip the leg squares from a glued-up slab consisting of three ¾ x 12 x 16-in. pieces, then dress the four sides to 2 in. square.

Since the legs are not set in a square relationship but rather rectangular, the cross stretchers must enter the legs at a corresponding angle. To determine the correct angle for the stretcher mortises, number the legs and stand them upright on a flat surface the proper distance apart. Place a straightedge diagonally across the center of the bevels of two facing legs and draw a line across the tops. Do the same with the other two legs. Now tilt your drill-press table to correspond with the cross lines on the legs and drill a series of ⅜-in. holes ⅜ in. deep in one pair of legs. Finally, do this for the others, tilting the table the other way.

Now build the top

To build the top, you'll have to edge-glue several boards and join them with dowels. Each butler-table hinge has a single-thickness leaf and a double-thickness one. It's standard to rout both mortises to suit the thicker leaf, then shim under the thin leaf. A bevel will have to be hand-chiseled at the outer edge of each mortise for hinge clearance.

If your router has a 5-in.-dia. base (most do), you can make your plywood hinge-mortising template the size given; if not, cut it to suit. Use the template's centerlines to position it over the hinge locations and place cardboard between the top and tray leaf for clearance. Then hold template, plus top and leaf, with C-clamps.

TILT THE DRILL-PRESS table so a pencil line on the leg and drill bit are vertical, then clamp.

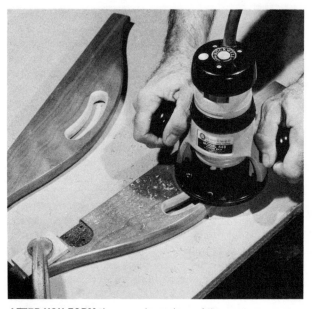

AFTER YOU FORM the curved openings of the built-in tray handles with a ¾-in. drill bit and sabre saw, use a router to carefully round the edges.

Folding snack server

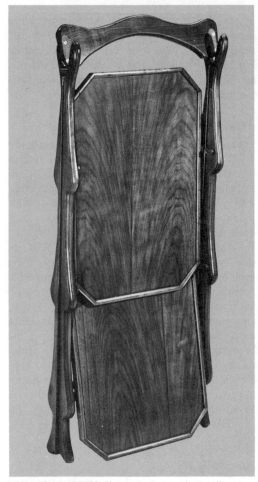

BETWEEN PARTIES, if you don't want it standing around, you can fold the server flat and stow it away. Trays lap and nest between the hinged legs.

■ WHEN HOME PARTIES reach the point of help yourself, this handsome hors d'oeuvre server will soon become the center of the party. Loaded with tempting cheese dips, chips and the makings of a drink or two, this self-service server will receive a standing ovation in more ways than one.

You'll find it equally as useful at bridge, or wherever snacks are served. Best of all, the server folds flat for storing. Start with the legs. These are twin assemblies which are cut in pairs, following the pattern. All four legs are bored for ¾-in.-dowel rungs, but keep in mind that the blind holes must be bored in facing surfaces. One pair of legs is drilled for four roundhead brass screws which serve as pivot-pins for the trays, and here you'll wisely drill the holes through both legs at the same time to insure identical spacing. If you own a router, run a bead cut along the curved edges of the legs; it will relieve their plainness and give that store-bought look.

One pair of legs is joined at the top with a crossrail which is shaped like the legs and then glued and screwed to the pair of legs previously drilled for the pivot screws. Two flathead screws are used at each end of the crossrail to fasten it.

Each tray consists of a hardwood-faced plywood center which is faced around the edge with a ¼ x ¾-in. molding, neatly mitered at the cor-

ners, then glued and nailed. Stop pins, made of nails with the heads cut off, are driven into the trays to rest in support blocks glued to the second pair of legs. The pins must not project so far that they rub and mar the legs. Wooden washers keep the trays from rubbing as they pivot for folding.

Pick small brass hinges to hinge the legs at the top. The hinge pins must be first driven out (if you can't get loose-pin hinges) so that the hinge leaves can be screwed in place. The pins are then replaced and your stand is completed.

Finishing the stand depends on the kind of wood you used. If it's walnut, you'll need to fill the open grain of the wood with a paste filler, then stain as desired. Two coats of rubbed-effect varnish will make a mighty handsome piece.

WHEN OPEN the sturdy server gives two generous-size surfaces for holding snacks and libations.

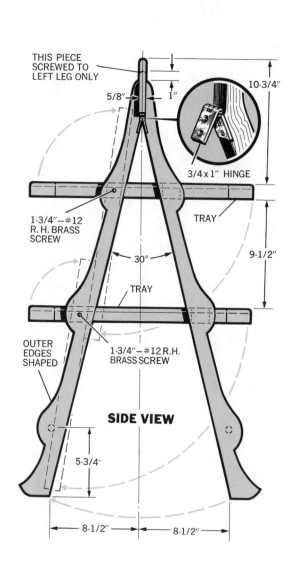

THIS PIECE
SCREWED TO
LEFT LEG ONLY

5/8″ — 1″

10-3/4″

3/4 x 1″ HINGE

1-3/4″—#12
R. H. BRASS
SCREW

TRAY

30°

9-1/2″

TRAY

1-3/4″—#12 R.H.
BRASS SCREW

OUTER
EDGES
SHAPED

SIDE VIEW

5-3/4″

8-1/2″   8-1/2″

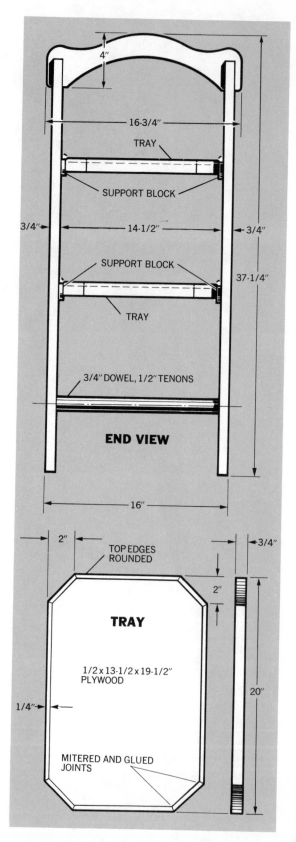

4″

16-3/4″

TRAY

SUPPORT BLOCK

3/4″   14-1/2″   3/4″

SUPPORT BLOCK

37-1/4″

TRAY

3/4″ DOWEL, 1/2″ TENONS

END VIEW

16″

2″   3/4″

TOP EDGES
ROUNDED

2″

TRAY

1/2 x 13-1/2 x 19-1/2″
PLYWOOD

1/4″

20″

MITERED AND GLUED
JOINTS

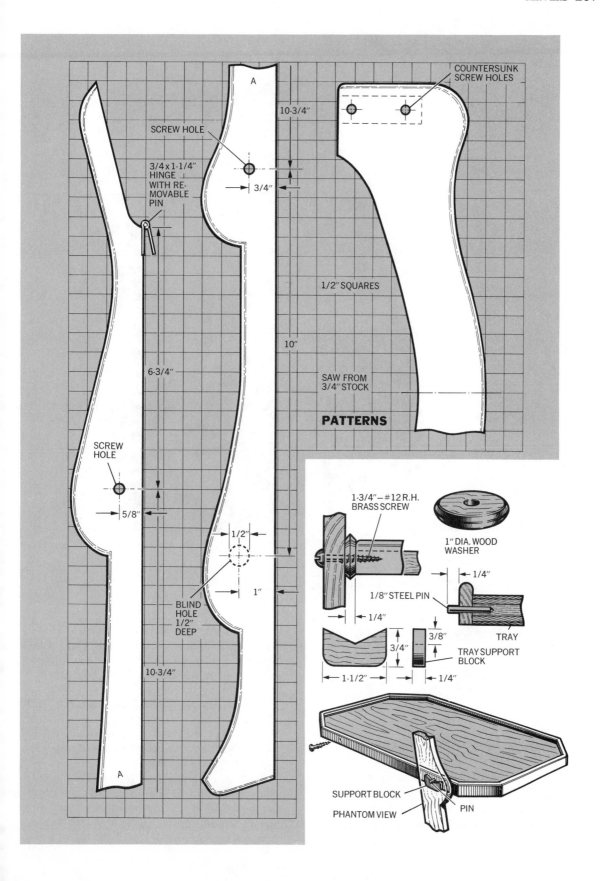

SCREW HOLE

3/4 x 1-1/4"
HINGE
WITH RE-
MOVABLE
PIN

A

10-3/4"

3/4"

COUNTERSUNK
SCREW HOLES

1/2" SQUARES

10"

SAW FROM
3/4" STOCK

PATTERNS

SCREW
HOLE

5/8"

6-3/4"

1/2"

1"

BLIND
HOLE
1/2"
DEEP

10-3/4"

A

1-3/4"—#12 R.H.
BRASS SCREW

1" DIA. WOOD
WASHER

1/4"

1/8" STEEL PIN

1/4"

1/4"

TRAY

3/8"

3/4"

TRAY SUPPORT
BLOCK

1-1/2"

1/4"

SUPPORT BLOCK

PHANTOM VIEW

PIN

Electric serving cart

■ THIS EARLY AMERICAN SERVING CART has a rich fruitwood finish, built-in electric warming tray, retractable cord, felt-lined silver and linen drawer and easy-rolling ball casters.

You'll need such special tools as a wood lathe and router, but don't worry about being an expert at finishing. Its slick finish is a decorative laminate—you just cement it on and that's it.

We covered the original cart with Colonial cherry and used solid cherry for the turned legs and exposed edges of the top, drop leaves, drawer fronts, lower shelf and front crossrails. These surfaces were later stained and finished to closely match the cherry laminate.

First turn the four legs from 1⅞-in. turning squares. To turn all four alike, make a full-size cardboard template to mark off the round and square sections of the leg. Mount each turning between centers so the top of the leg is at the headstock end of the lathe. This way, with a bit in the tailstock, you'll be able to bore holes dead-center in the ends of the legs for casters.

Next cut the four end aprons. The two top ones are 5¼ in. wide; the two bottom ones are 4⅜ in. Cover the aprons with laminate before you trim them to size and bore the dowel holes. The upper aprons are kept even with the tops of the legs and 3/16 in. in from the face. The lower aprons are ¾ in. from being centered on the square portion of the leg to allow for the bottom shelf which rests on them. Now dowel and glue the aprons to the legs. Cover and cut the top and bottom back aprons to size and bore for dowels. They're 26¼ in. long and the same widths as the end aprons, set in the same amount and cut from fir plywood.

The recessed front apron is built up as shown in section A-A. Top and bottom rails of cherry are glued and nailed to a center piece of ½-in. fir plywood. Then a filler block of cherry is glued to the front to divide the recessed apron exactly in half. The ends are bored for dowels as before to align with holes in the legs. The top surface of the top rail is later covered with laminate so the lid will be flush with the rest when closed.

Cut the lower crossrail 26¼ in. long from cherry and bore for dowels. Now glue the parts to the end assemblies. Do this at one time, preferably with clamps. Keep the assembly square.

While the glue is drying, make the recessed shelf for the warming tray (Detail A). It consists of a ¾-in. fir-plywood panel with a hole in it to fit the flanged tray. Two ¾-in.-square cleats are glued to the front and back edges, and two ¾ x 1¾-in. members are glued on edge at the ends. (Here it's wise to check the 14¹³/₁₆-in. dimension against the actual inside width of the cart.)

LEG

Square	5-3/4"
Round	12"
Square	5-3/4"
Round	3"

1-7/8"
1-1/4"
1-1/2"
26-1/2"
1-1/8"
7/8"
1-3/8"

SERVING CART

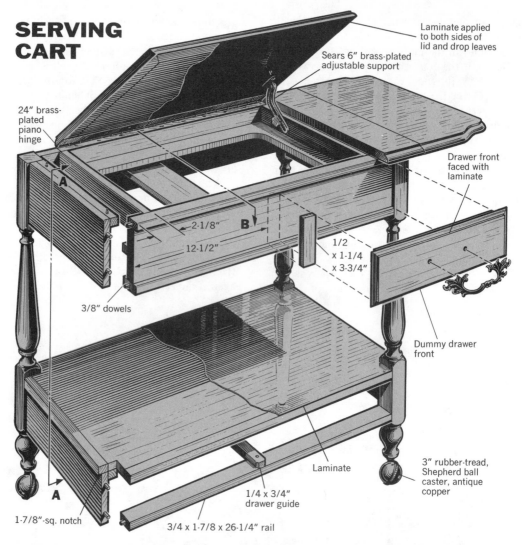

Laminate applied to both sides of lid and drop leaves

Sears 6" brass-plated adjustable support

24" brass-plated piano hinge

Drawer front faced with laminate

2-1/8"

B

12-1/2"

1/2 x 1-1/4 x 3-3/4"

3/8" dowels

Dummy drawer front

Laminate

3" rubber-tread, Shepherd ball caster, antique copper

1/4 x 3/4" drawer guide

3/4 x 1-7/8 x 26-1/4" rail

A

1-7/8"-sq. notch

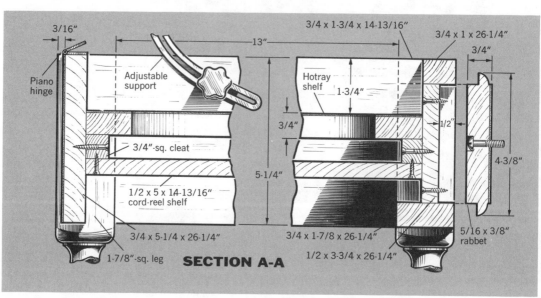

3/16"

Piano hinge

13"

Adjustable support

3/4 x 1-3/4 x 14-13/16"

3/4 x 1 x 26-1/4"

3/4"

Hotray shelf

1-3/4"

3/4"

1/2"

3/4"-sq. cleat

1/2 x 5 x 14-13/16" cord-reel shelf

5-1/4"

4-3/8"

3/4 x 5-1/4 x 26-1/4"

3/4 x 1-7/8 x 26-1/4"

5/16 x 3/8" rabbet

1-7/8"-sq. leg

SECTION A-A

1/2 x 3-3/4 x 26-1/4"

Since the tray shelf is also faced with laminate, it's easier to cover it before it's installed. We covered the shelf top and inside surfaces of the ends with yellow laminate. After installing it, we added 1¾-in.-wide strips of the laminate to exposed parts of the aprons. The ½ x 5-in. cross-member, screwed to the shelf cleats, supports the self-winding cord reel.

To make the bottom shelf, glue ¾ x 1-in. strips of cherry to the edges of a plywood center panel, notch the corners for legs and cover the top with laminate. Attach the completed shelf to the cart with screws through cleats glued to the end aprons. (Study section B-B.)

Make the lid, top and drop-leaf parts essentially the same way, but make the edge pieces 1½ in. wide and miter the corners. Note that the narrow top sections are banded only on three edges. Both top and bottom surfaces of the five top parts are covered with laminate, then the edges are shaped. Use a standard drop-leaf cutter and its mate to shape the hinged edges. The other edges can be shaped with less of a shoulder or even with a different-shaped cutter. Mortise the drop-leaf table hinges flush with the laminate. Be sure the barrels of the hinges are centered exactly on the shoulder of the shaped edge.

Attach the narrow top sections to the cart with cleats and screws from below and let them overhang the ends 1⅜ in. The lid should fit between the two with ¹/₁₆-in. clearance at each side. It's hinged at the back with a piano hinge mortised flush with the laminate. The lid should overhang front and back ¾ in. Adding an adjustable sup-

Section B-B diagram:

4-3/4"
1-3/8"
Plastic laminate
3/8"
2-1/4"
1-3/4"
Plastic laminate
3/4"-sq. cleat across back apron
3/4 x 5-1/4 x 26-1/4"
3/4 x 5-1/4 x 13" end apron
drop-leaf bracket

SECTION B-B

3/4" lumber-core plywood
Filler strip
3/4" cleat
Plastic laminate
4-3/8"
1/4"
3/4" cleat across back rail
Drawer guide cleat

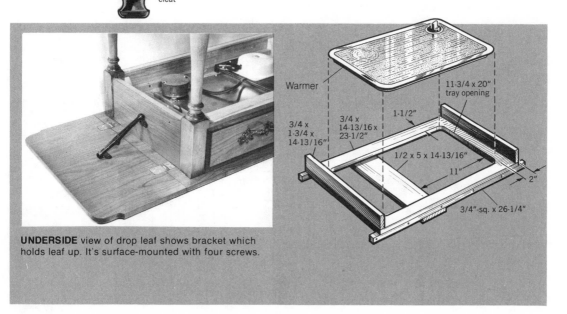

UNDERSIDE view of drop leaf shows bracket which holds leaf up. It's surface-mounted with four screws.

Warmer
11-3/4 x 20" tray opening
1-1/2"
3/4 x 1-3/4 x 14-13/16"
3/4 x 14-13/16 x 23-1/2"
1/2 x 5 x 14-13/16"
11"
2"
3/4"-sq. x 26-1/4"

port like the one shown completes the lid. Fit the drop leaves with surface-mounted, spring-loaded brackets.

The drawers complete the job. The two upper ones are dummies, of course; they're actually made and attached before laminate is applied to the inside of the tray shelf. The fronts are pieces of cherry, rabbeted around the back, faced with laminate and shaped. Attach the pulls before you screw the fronts in place.

Make the front of the bottom drawer as just described, and the rest is typical drawer assembly (see construction details, below). Attach a grooved guide to the bottom to ride on a rail screwed to the front crossrail and to a cleat added to the back apron. Note in section B-B how drawer rubrails are nailed to the end aprons.

Wire the plug-in cord reel to a junction box mounted on the tray bottom. Use wire suited for 167° F, and be sure the tray is properly grounded.

A RETRACTABLE REEL, which holds 6 ft. of cord, is wired to the junction box that comes with the tray.

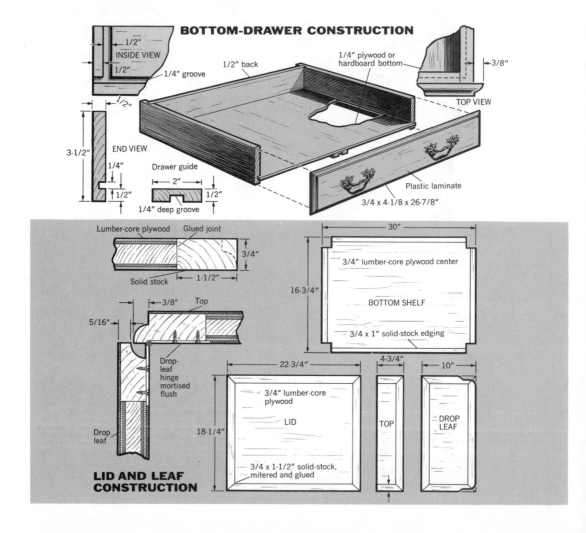

BOTTOM-DRAWER CONSTRUCTION

INSIDE VIEW — 1/2", 1/2", 1/4" groove
1/2" back
1/4" plywood or hardboard bottom
TOP VIEW — 3/8"
END VIEW — 1/2", 3-1/2", 1/4", 1/2"
Drawer guide — 2", 1/2", 1/4" deep groove
Plastic laminate
3/4 x 4-1/8 x 26-7/8"

LID AND LEAF CONSTRUCTION

Lumber-core plywood — Glued joint — 3/4"
Solid stock — 1-1/2"

Top — 3/8", 5/16"
Drop-leaf hinge mortised flush
Drop leaf

30"
3/4" lumber-core plywood center
16-3/4"
BOTTOM SHELF
3/4 x 1" solid-stock edging

22-3/4"
4-3/4"
10"
3/4" lumber-core plywood
LID
TOP
DROP LEAF
18-1/4"
3/4 x 1-1/2" solid-stock, mitered and glued

DRAWER SLIDES on single glide mounted on shelf center. Cabinet sides are let into the blind dadoes in top.

Early American server

■ THIS VERSION of an early American server is a handsome piece of furniture that offers well-organized storage space and occupies little floor area. It has the look of old-world craftsmanship.

Easy to build with power tools, the cabinet offers these advantages:
● Plaques "carved" of plastic look, and can be worked, like real wood.
● Hardware for bypassing doors is concealed (there's no bottom track to clean out) and places the doors in a flush position when they are closed.

In building the prototype, we made sure that all door stiles and rails would reveal 2 in. (in closed position). Thus, you'll notice in the drawing that these sizes vary because of the bevel cuts and the cabinet stiles and rails.

The cabinet. To start, cut all pieces to size.

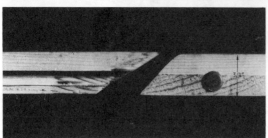

HOW THE HARDWARE WORKS . . .

SLIDING DOORS bypass with the left-hand door (facing the cabinet) always remaining in front, no matter which door is moved. Bottom view of doors (left) shows a groove needed for the track that goes on the left door. A plunger (below, left) and guide pin (not visible) are only hardware in the cabinet bottom. Left door slides on the pin, corner brace acts as a stop. Bottom view shows shelf bottom and hardware mounted in cabinet on doors. Glide on shelf is for the drawer.

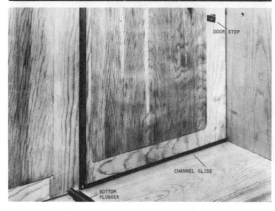
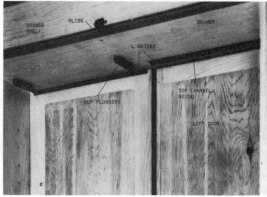

They'll make quite a pile, so label each piece lightly with a soft pencil for easy identification later. Make certain that you kerf the underside of the drawer shelf before you go farther. This kerf is needed for the top rail and, should you forget it, would be a time-consuming task by hand after the cabinet is assembled.

It is good practice to tack the pieces together temporarily, using diagonal braces on the back to keep it in square. When satisfied with cabinet fit, you can assemble the drawer and doors using the cabinet for final determination of their measurements.

The drawer is simply a box made of ½-in. pine.

Because it is shallow, ⅛-in. hardboard is adequate for the bottom, which is let into dadoes. The false drawer front is ¾-in. pine, and with the saw blade set as shown, the raised panel is quickly made. Bevel ends first, then cut the lengths.

The doors are a little trickier, mostly because of the varying stile and rail widths. You may find it easiest to lay out both doors on the workbench and, after marking, shiplapping one stile or rail at a time. The ¼-in. plywood panels are let into a rabbet; the decorative plaques, glued to the fronts, are of molded plastic. Because the hardware will not permit a door thickness greater than ¾ in. (or the doors won't bypass), these had to be reduced in thickness. The plaques are attached with adhesive.

The hardware. You pay a slight price—in labor—for the beauty this hardware offers. It *is* harder to install than conventional sliding-door hardware and will likely call for a little trial-and-error fitting. The hardware package has a template. Once the cabinet was completely finished (varnished), however, a quick blast of spray silicone made the doors bypass effortlessly.

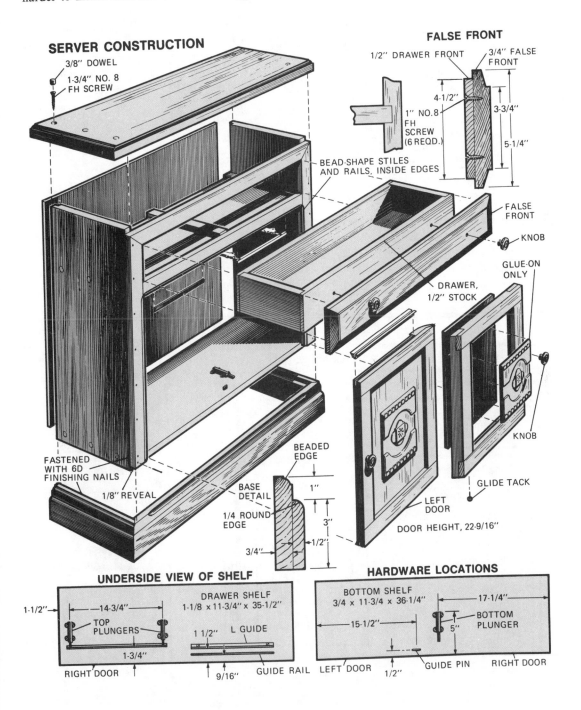

SERVER CONSTRUCTION

3/8" DOWEL
1-3/4" NO. 8 FH SCREW

BEAD-SHAPE STILES AND RAILS, INSIDE EDGES

FASTENED WITH 6D FINISHING NAILS

1/8" REVEAL

BASE DETAIL

BEADED EDGE
1"
1/4 ROUND EDGE
3"
3/4"
1/2"

FALSE FRONT

1/2" DRAWER FRONT
3/4" FALSE FRONT
4-1/2"
3-3/4"
1" NO.8 FH SCREW (6 REQD.)
5-1/4"

FALSE FRONT

KNOB

DRAWER, 1/2" STOCK

GLUE-ON ONLY

KNOB

GLIDE TACK

LEFT DOOR

DOOR HEIGHT, 22-9/16"

UNDERSIDE VIEW OF SHELF

1-1/2"
14-3/4"
TOP PLUNGERS
1-3/4"
RIGHT DOOR

DRAWER SHELF 1-1/8 x 11-3/4" x 35-1/2"

1 1/2"   L GUIDE
9/16"   GUIDE RAIL

HARDWARE LOCATIONS

BOTTOM SHELF 3/4 x 11-3/4 x 36-1/4"
17-1/4"
15-1/2"
BOTTOM PLUNGER
5"
LEFT DOOR
1/2"
GUIDE PIN
RIGHT DOOR

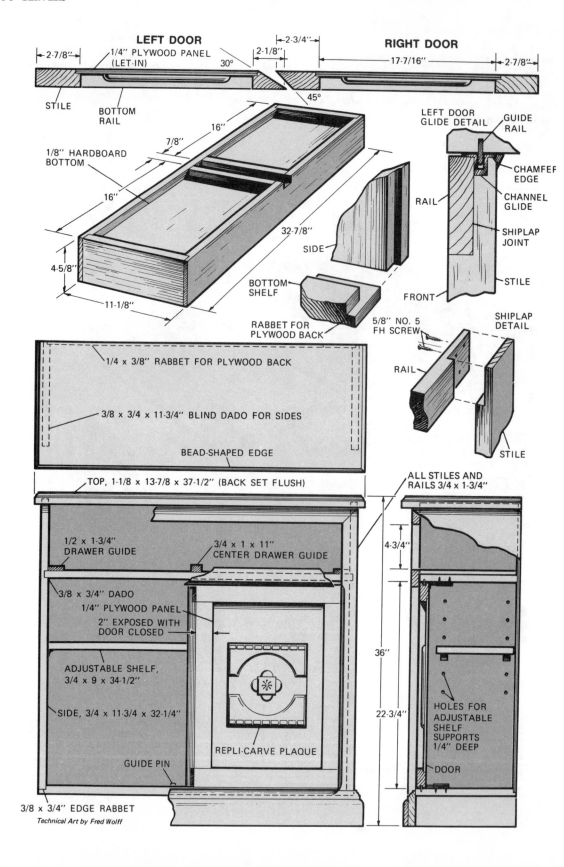

LEFT DOOR

2-7/8"

1/4" PLYWOOD PANEL (LET-IN)

30°

2-3/4"

2-1/8"

RIGHT DOOR

17-7/16"

2-7/8"

STILE

BOTTOM RAIL

45°

LEFT DOOR GLIDE DETAIL

GUIDE RAIL

16"

7/8"

1/8" HARDBOARD BOTTOM

16"

32-7/8"

SIDE

RAIL

CHAMFER EDGE

CHANNEL GLIDE

SHIPLAP JOINT

STILE

4-5/8"

11-1/8"

BOTTOM SHELF

RABBET FOR PLYWOOD BACK

5/8" NO. 5 FH SCREW

FRONT

SHIPLAP DETAIL

RAIL

1/4 x 3/8" RABBET FOR PLYWOOD BACK

3/8 x 3/4 x 11-3/4" BLIND DADO FOR SIDES

BEAD-SHAPED EDGE

STILE

TOP, 1-1/8 x 13-7/8 x 37-1/2" (BACK SET FLUSH)

ALL STILES AND RAILS 3/4 x 1-3/4"

1/2 x 1-3/4" DRAWER GUIDE

3/4 x 1 x 11" CENTER DRAWER GUIDE

4-3/4"

3/8 x 3/4" DADO

1/4" PLYWOOD PANEL

2" EXPOSED WITH DOOR CLOSED

36"

ADJUSTABLE SHELF, 3/4 x 9 x 34-1/2"

SIDE, 3/4 x 11-3/4 x 32-1/4"

REPLI-CARVE PLAQUE

22-3/4"

HOLES FOR ADJUSTABLE SHELF SUPPORTS 1/4" DEEP

DOOR

GUIDE PIN

3/8 x 3/4" EDGE RABBET

Technical Art by Fred Wolff

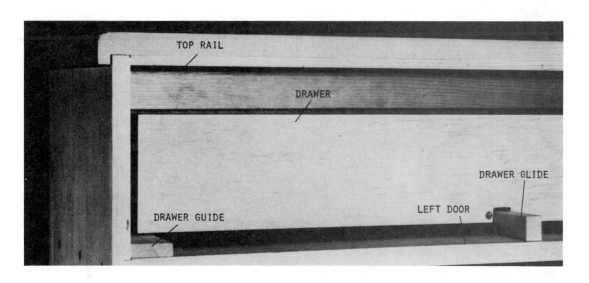

TOP RAIL

DRAWER

DRAWER GLIDE

LEFT DOOR

DRAWER GUIDE

CUSTOMIZING THE PLAQUES

CUT DOWN the plaques to assure that door thickness will not exceed ¾ in. You can start by trimming four sides (right).

TRIM DECORATIVE nubs (below, left) so doors will bypass easily. When doors are in place, use belt sander to remove high spots.

PLAQUES, before and after trimming (below, right). Views of finished cabinet show that trimming doesn't hurt appearance.

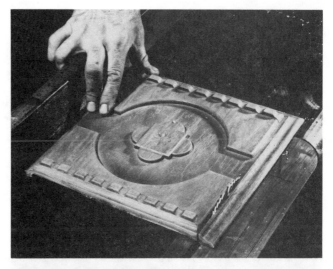

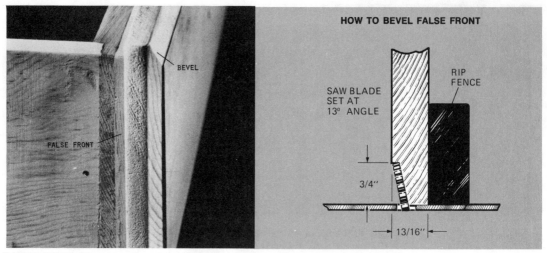

RAISED-PANEL effect is easily accomplished on a table saw; false front is then glued to the drawer.

Assembly. The cabinet top and sides are assembled using screws and dowel plugs. All other assembly is accomplished with well-set finishing nails. The holes can be filled, but for an antique look, they were not on the server shown.

Finish. After thorough sanding, wipe the server with a tack cloth and apply oil stain. Wipe off excess stain and let dry overnight. Next day, antique the server using a tube of burnt umber and a rag to darken those areas that are dark on actual antiques. Use the rag to blend all dark spots into adjacent stain.

Coat the plaques with red enamel, allow to dry and antique the same way as before using a flat black enamel.

Finally, give the entire piece three coats of varnish. You can, if desired, let the final coat cure for three or four weeks and then apply Butcher's Wax.

HARDWARE for the pair of sliding doors is shown below. It is also available for four-door cabinets.

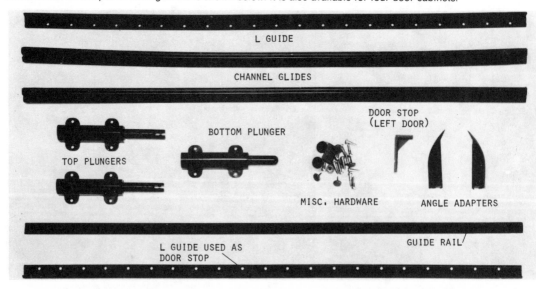

Lazy Susan table server

■ YOU DON'T NEED a lathe to make this handsome lazy Susan table server. You can buy the 12 little gallery spindles already turned at many lumberyards.

The circular base is cut from a glued-up square of cherry ¾ x 18 x 18 in. You make it by cutting four triangular segments from a 10-in. board with the miter gauge set at 45° and flipping the board for each pass. The butting edges of the four segments are shaped with a glue-joint cutter, or drilled for dowels. The glued-up square will have lateral-running grain of interesting symmetry and good workability when you're ready to shape it. Note the use of C-clamps and bar clamps to hold the work while glue dries.

The stock for the upper ring is glued-up the same way, but to economize on lumber, the segments need not be full triangles; they may be truncated. Cut them from a 6-in. board to the same measurements you used for the base. When the four are joined, you will have an 18-in. square with a square opening in the center. When sabre-sawing the ring, you'll have to insert a piece of scrap stock across the center of the opening to provide a surface for the saw's pivot point. This can be toenailed in place. Be sure to saw the outer circle of the ring first. Use a router or shaper to mold the edges.

Alignment of the spindle holes will be easy if you tape the ring to the base and drill the holes from the bottom side of the base and partly into the underside of the ring. Make an identifying mark on both pieces so they can later be matched as they were when drilled.

A worthwhile tip: Sand the parts and apply the finish before assembling your server for a top-notch job. A coat of sanding sealer followed with stain and a final coat or two of clear satin finish will give you a smooth handsome finish that will last for many years.

To complete the project, you'll need a 4-in. lazy Susan bearing. Attach this to a piece of wood scrap ½ x 9 x 9 in. Drill a 1-in.-dia. screw access hole in this subbase, attach the bearing and then screw the unit to the circular base.

FOUR TRIANGULAR segments for circular base are ready for jointing butted edges prior to gluing.

C-CLAMPS ARE USED at corners; bar clamp applies pressure to the center area of glued-up work.

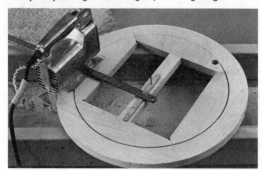

OUTER CUT of ring is made first to preserve support for the saw's pivot when making inside cut.

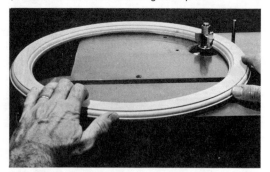

COLLAR CONTROLS depth of cut when you shape edges with a shaper; you can also use a router.

PILOT HOLES for spindles are drilled in base and ring at the same time to assure perfect alignment.

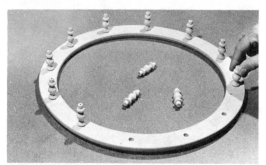

READY-MADE spindles fit ⅜-in. holes. They are not glued until finishing has been completed.

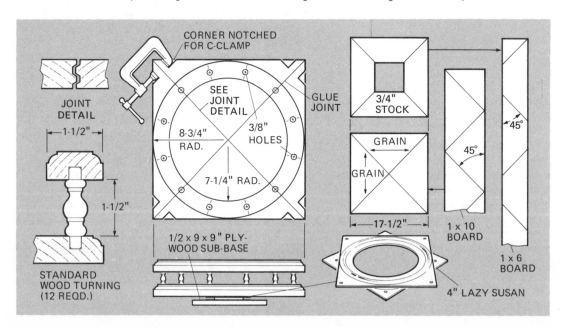

JOINT DETAIL

1-1/2"

1-1/2"

STANDARD WOOD TURNING (12 REQD.)

CORNER NOTCHED FOR C-CLAMP

SEE JOINT DETAIL

8-3/4" RAD.

3/8" HOLES

7-1/4" RAD.

GLUE JOINT

1/2 x 9 x 9" PLY-WOOD SUB-BASE

3/4" STOCK

GRAIN

GRAIN

17-1/2"

45°

45°

1 x 10 BOARD

1 x 6 BOARD

4" LAZY SUSAN

Sewing center for every taste and need

■ LIKE ANY HOBBY, sewing becomes more enjoyable and creates a lot less clutter when you have a work center where there's a place for everything and everything is in one convenient place.

We kept this thought in mind in designing these four highly functional sewing centers. Incorporated in each design you'll find a work counter for pattern cutting, shelves and roomy drawers for keeping fabrics, yarns and patterns handy and trays for pins, needles and threads. Two of the centers are designed to attach to a wall; all fold up in a minimum of space.

Most sewing-machine stands we've seen are just that—stands for sewing machines. They provide a place to store the machine when it's not in use and that's about all. Few, if any, offer a good-size worktable to spread out a pattern. There's little space to keep dress patterns handy. There's no space to stow your sewing and often a lack of tray space to hold countless little items. We've tried to give you these features that most stands lack.

Any portable-type sewing machine is adaptable to any of the four centers shown here. The counter cutouts were made to fit a particular base. While a cutout allows the machine to sit flush, this can be optional; the machine can simply sit on top of the counter. Plans and instructions for building all four of these sewing centers are shown on the following pages.

THE HIGH-RISE UNIT

Emphasizing convenience, this sewing center is built around three 1⅜-in. flush doors, one left intact and the others cut into sections. The boxlike case to which they are hinged and pivoted is divided into three compartments.

To make the case, cut two side members 13¼ x 84¾ in., then cut a ⅜ x ¾-in. rabbet in the top edges and ⅜ x ¾-in. dadoes 2¼ in. up from the bottom. The rabbets are for a 13 x 76-in. top member; the dadoes for a 13 x 76-in. bottom member. A ¼-in. plywood back laps the edges of top and bottom members, but fits in rabbets cut in the edges of the two side members. The two partitions, 13 x 81 in., are nailed in place through top and bottom members. The left partition is positioned 25¼ in. from the outside; the right one, 23¼ in.

Front edges of the case are faced with 1⅛ x 1½-in. trim pieces of pine, with a 3-in.-wide piece across the bottom. Details B and C in the drawings show how the trim is kept flush with inner faces of the two partitions. Casing nails are used to attach the trim, and the heads are set and puttied.

The left-hand compartment is fitted with a stock 22x80-in. flush door hinged with regular 3-in. door butts. The opening as dimensioned provides ⅛-in. door clearance all around. A rabbeted stop is on the full length of the door (see detail B); similar stops are on both right-hand doors; the upper stop being 29¾ in. long, the lower one 13⅞ in. The upper right compartment has a ¾-in. bottom 31½ in. down from the top, and a 1½-in. trim piece covers the edge.

The 28-in. center door is cut in two sections at a point 64½ in. from one end. Since interior doors are hollow, filler strips of solid wood must be inserted and glued in the cut ends. The 64½-in. section is the cutting board and is covered on the back with plastic laminate.

The 20-in. right-hand door is cut in three sections: 29¾, 34½ and 13⅞ in. The 34½-in. section is a swing-up sewing-machine counter. To provide a well for the base of the machine, the

THE ULTIMATE in sewing centers, this one opens up to offer maximum convenience. Standing 7 ft. tall, it features a closet for storing an iron and ironing board, a swing-down 28x64½-in. cutting board, a leg-free, pull-down sewing machine, a mirror door and more storage than you'll ever need. Three common interior doors are used for the front; the rest is chiefly plywood. When tipped on side, the cabinet will easily pass through any standard-height doorway.

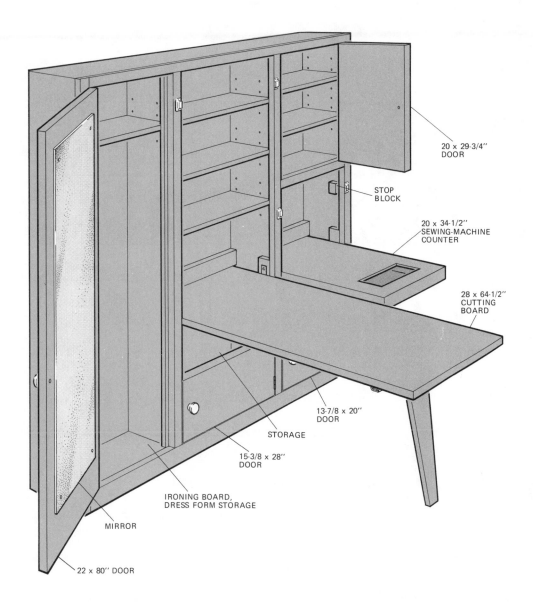

20 x 29-3/4''
DOOR

STOP
BLOCK

20 x 34-1/2''
SEWING-MACHINE
COUNTER

28 x 64-1/2''
CUTTING
BOARD

13-7/8 x 20''
DOOR

STORAGE

15-3/8 x 28''
DOOR

IRONING BOARD,
DRESS FORM STORAGE

MIRROR

22 x 80'' DOOR

counter must be double-thick as shown in the detail, after which the top surface and the three exposed edges of the sandwich are covered with plastic laminate.

Modified mending plates and ¼-20 T-nuts are used to pivot the cutting board and machine counter. As shown, the plates are attached to the edges, 12½ in. from the far end in the case of the cutting board, 12⅞ in. for the counter. T-nuts are installed in ⁵/₁₆-in. holes in the cabinet at points 29⅜ in. up from the bottom for the counter and 31¼ for the cutting table. Both sets of holes are

drilled 1¾ in. in from the edge. Roundhead stovebolts are turned through the T-nuts from the outside, through the pivot holes in the mending plates and on into holes in the edges of the counter and cutting board. Bolts 2½ in. long are required for the machine counter, 1 in. long for the cutting board.

A stop block across the back supports the counter in a level position when it's down, and regular cupboard catches are used to hold the cutting board and sewing-machine counter when up. Friction catches hold the four doors shut. A

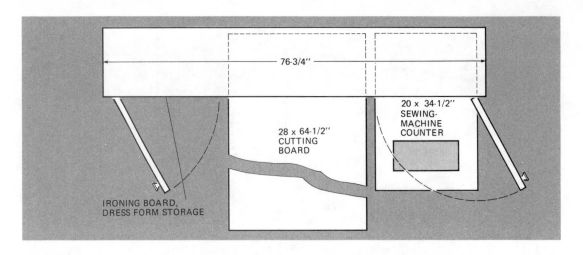

76-3/4''

28 x 64-1/2''
CUTTING
BOARD

20 x 34-1/2''
SEWING-
MACHINE
COUNTER

IRONING BOARD,
DRESS FORM STORAGE

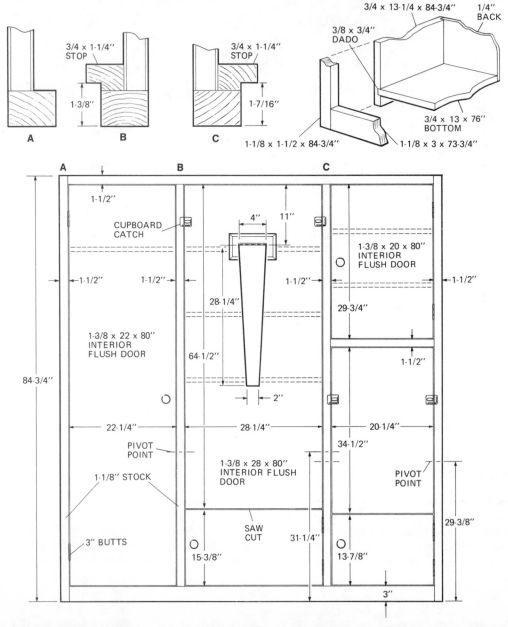

3/4 x 1-1/4''
STOP

1-3/8''

3/4 x 1-1/4''
STOP

1-7/16''

3/4 x 13-1/4 x 84-3/4''

1/4''
BACK

3/8 x 3/4''
DADO

3/4 x 13 x 76''
BOTTOM

1-1/8 x 1-1/2 x 84-3/4''

1-1/8 x 3 x 73-3/4''

A

B

C

A

B

C

1-1/2''

CUPBOARD
CATCH

4''

11''

1-3/8 x 20 x 80''
INTERIOR
FLUSH DOOR

1-1/2''

1-1/2''

1-1/2''

28-1/4''

29-3/4''

1-1/2''

1-1/2''

1-3/8 x 22 x 80''
INTERIOR
FLUSH DOOR

84-3/4''

64-1/2''

1-1/2''

2''

22-1/4''

28-1/4''

20-1/4''

PIVOT
POINT

34-1/2''

PIVOT
POINT

1-1/8'' STOCK

1-3/8 x 28 x 80''
INTERIOR FLUSH
DOOR

29-3/8''

3'' BUTTS

SAW
CUT

31-1/4''

15-3/8''

13-7/8''

3''

swing-down leg hinged to a block glued to the front of the cutting board supports it. All shelves are adjustable; more can be added.

The method used to hold the machine securely in the counter cutout so it can be swung up depends on your particular machine and its base. One way to fasten it would be to drill four small holes through the metal base; countersink them and drive nickel-plated oval-head wood screws into the plywood top.

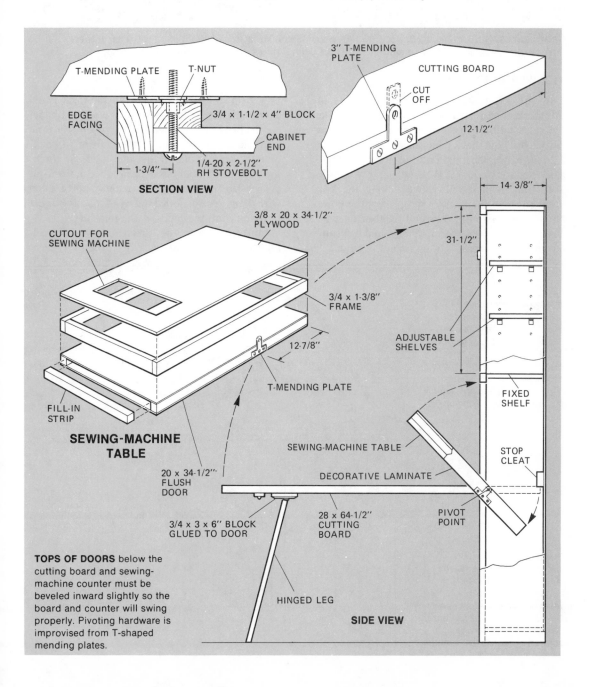

SECTION VIEW

T-MENDING PLATE   T-NUT
EDGE FACING
3/4 x 1-1/2 x 4" BLOCK
CABINET END
1-3/4"
1/4-20 x 2-1/2" RH STOVEBOLT

3" T-MENDING PLATE
CUTTING BOARD
CUT OFF
12-1/2"

SEWING-MACHINE TABLE

CUTOUT FOR SEWING MACHINE
3/8 x 20 x 34-1/2" PLYWOOD
3/4 x 1-3/8" FRAME
12-7/8"
T-MENDING PLATE
FILL-IN STRIP

20 x 34-1/2" FLUSH DOOR
3/4 x 3 x 6" BLOCK GLUED TO DOOR

SEWING-MACHINE TABLE
DECORATIVE LAMINATE
28 x 64-1/2" CUTTING BOARD
HINGED LEG

14- 3/8"
31-1/2"
ADJUSTABLE SHELVES
FIXED SHELF
STOP CLEAT
PIVOT POINT

SIDE VIEW

TOPS OF DOORS below the cutting board and sewing-machine counter must be beveled inward slightly so the board and counter will swing properly. Pivoting hardware is improvised from T-shaped mending plates.

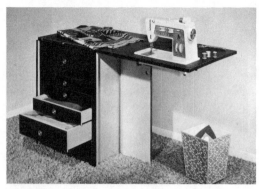 

DROP LEAVES on island unit swing up to provide a whopping work surface nearly 84 in. long. Five center drawers offer storage space galore. Sewing machine fits in the cutout, stores in compartment under the hinged lid.

THE ISLAND UNIT

In checking the construction details of this work center, you'll see that you can make the sides with ¼ or ¾-in. plywood. Begin by cutting the ¾-in. back panel. It will be 22¾ in. or 23¼ in. wide, depending on the plywood thickness used for the sides. Where ¼-in. plywood is used, run ⅜-in.-deep grooves along the two outer edges of the back ⅞ in. in from the edge. Next cut the two top rails and front pilasters—1⅜ or 1⅝ in., as the case may be—and run similar grooves in them ⅞ in. in from the edge.

A ¾-in.-thick bottom nails to the back panel even with the bottom edge, and a second panel (½ in. thick) is installed 8¼ in. down from the top. The latter is ¾ in. shorter, front to back, than the bottom one. If the sides are ¼ in. thick, the bottom member has to be notched at the front corners to fit around the pilasters and be even with them. You'll notice the two top rails project ½ in. beyond the faces of the pilasters.

Start assembling the parts you have cut, nailing the bottom to the back first, then the ½-in.

COMPARTMENT under lid provides storage space for portable machine. Bin at rear is handy for filing patterns. Cutout in counter is optional; the machine can rest on top if you desire. Use friction-type lid support; it helps to hold up the lid when storing machine.

SHADED AREAS show the surfaces to face with plastic laminate if you wish only to cover the parts that are exposed when the cabinet is fully closed. Other surfaces can be painted or stained either in matching or contrasting colors. Use furniture glides under corners, wings.

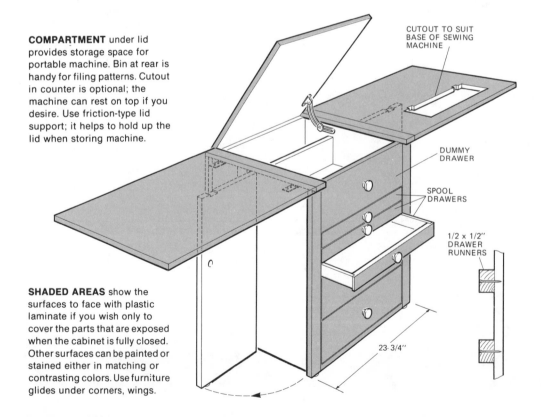

CUTOUT TO SUIT BASE OF SEWING MACHINE

DUMMY DRAWER

SPOOL DRAWERS

1/2 x 1/2" DRAWER RUNNERS

23-3/4"

bottom, followed in order by the sides, top rails and pilasters. If you plan to cover the parts with plastic laminate, you won't have to worry about nailheads showing. If not, you'll have to set and putty the nails that show in the top rails and pilasters.

The 8¾-in. dummy drawer front is cut and fitted next. Notice that it is held in place with glue blocks on the inside, and that it fits even with the bottom member. We found it easier to apply the plastic laminate to the face of it before gluing it in place. Notice how the laminate (see section B-B) is cut back ¹/₁₆ in. at each end to simulate normal drawer clearance. A 6-in.-wide partition, either 20 or 20½ in. long, as the case

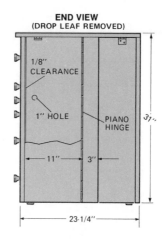

END VIEW
(DROP LEAF REMOVED)

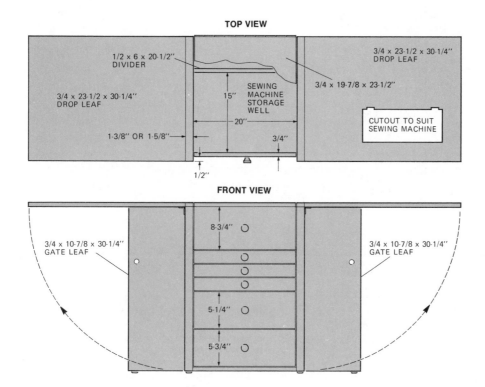

TOP VIEW

1/2 x 6 x 20-1/2"
DIVIDER

3/4 x 23-1/2 x 30-1/4"
DROP LEAF

3/4 x 23-1/2 x 30-1/4"
DROP LEAF

3/4 x 19-7/8 x 23-1/2"

SEWING MACHINE STORAGE WELL

15"

20"

1-3/8" OR 1-5/8"

3/4"

1/2"

CUTOUT TO SUIT SEWING MACHINE

FRONT VIEW

8-3/4"

5-1/4"

5-3/4"

3/4 x 10-7/8 x 30-1/4"
GATE LEAF

3/4 x 10-7/8 x 30-1/4"
GATE LEAF

may be, is installed in the machine compartment 15 in. from the front and nailed in through the sides.

Supporting wings for drop leaves are hinged to ¾ x 3-in. vertical members, added to recessed sides of the cabinet 11 in. back from the front. Finger holes are made an inch or so in from the front edges of the wings, and a notch is made in the top of each one so that it will clear the front

hinges. Allow a ⅛-in. space for clearance at the cabinet front so that the wings will swing out easily.

Cut the hinged top 19⅞ in. wide and use a piano hinge to attach it securely across the back. Complete it with a friction-lid support. Hinge the two drop leaves, then place the cabinet on its back and drive rubber-cushion furniture glides into the four corners and outer ends of the wings.

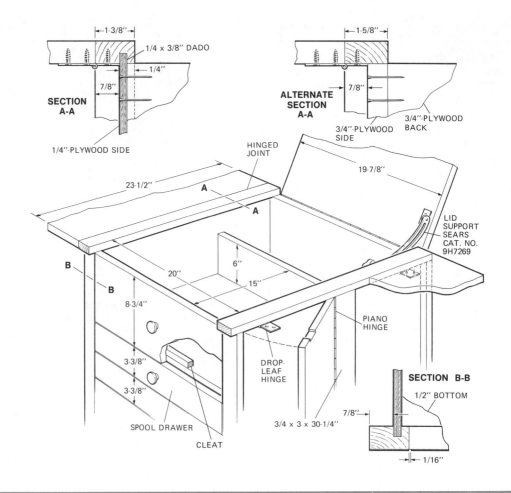

1-3/8"
1/4 x 3/8" DADO
1/4"
7/8"

SECTION A-A

1/4"-PLYWOOD SIDE

1-5/8"
7/8"

ALTERNATE SECTION A-A

3/4"-PLYWOOD SIDE

3/4"-PLYWOOD BACK

HINGED JOINT

23-1/2"

19-7/8"

A

A

LID SUPPORT SEARS CAT. NO. 9H7269

B

B

6"

20"

15"

8-3/4"

PIANO HINGE

3-3/8"

3-3/8"

DROP-LEAF HINGE

SECTION B-B

1/2" BOTTOM

7/8"

SPOOL DRAWER

CLEAT

3/4 x 3 x 30-1/4"

1/16"

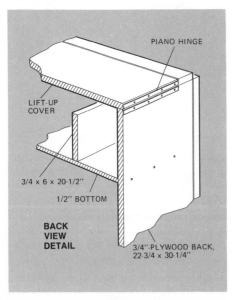

PIANO HINGE

LIFT-UP COVER

3/4 x 6 x 20-1/2"

1/2" BOTTOM

BACK VIEW DETAIL

3/4"-PLYWOOD BACK, 22-3/4 x 30-1/4"

CEMENTING PLASTIC LAMINATE

1. Cut your laminate 1/8 in. oversize all around.
2. Surfaces to be bonded must be dry and clean.
3. Apply even coat of contact cement to both laminate and wood, using brush or spreader.
4. Let both surfaces dry before bonding (10-20 minutes normally). Surfaces will bond when adhesive will adhere but not transfer to brown wrapping paper if touched lightly. If cement becomes too dry (over 3 hours), apply another coat.
5. Bring surfaces in contact *exactly* where desired (cement bonds instantly on contact, so you can't shift the work later). Two over-lapping pieces of kraft paper placed over cement will let you position the laminate without sticking. When laminate is where you want it, pull out one paper, press down the plastic, then pull out second paper.
6. Using rubber mallet or hammer and wood block, apply pressure all over surface for positive contact.
7. Trim laminate flush with work; use block plane and flat file or router and special laminate cutter.
8. Clean tools, brushes with contact-cement solvent.

THE DUAL UNIT

Simplest to make of the four sewing centers is a dual-unit center that appeals to the builder who wants to spend a minimum of time and money. Of its two individual units, one is attached to the wall to accommodate a portable sewing machine and the other is placed alongside. Together they offer the sewer convenience and storage galore.

Little more than a box fitted with a back and shelves, the drop-counter wall unit is practically a hammer and saw project. The ends and the top and bottom members are cut in pairs as are the four shelves. The top and bottom boards lap the end members, and the two long shelves butt between. To gain "headroom" for nailing the short divider in place, you should install the lower long shelf first, then the two short shelves and finally the upper one. Chains support the drop front; hooks and eyes hold it shut. Two 3-in. angle brackets across the top and bottom

anchor the unit solidly to wall studs.

Although the base unit is twice as deep as the wall unit, construction is much the same. The top and bottom members lap the end members, and a divider forms compartments. One difference you'll notice in basic construction is the 1½-in. apron that's let in across the front at the top. This requires ¾ x 1½-in. notches cut before assembly.

The sit-down ironing board pivots on a single carriage bolt that passes through a hole in the second shelf and swings clear of the end when not in use. Two drawers with handholds are made to slide easily in the 12 and 22½-in. openings. Stock cabinet louvers are used for doors and trimmed to fit. They're hinged to fold, and held shut by magnetic catches.

The wall unit should be hung so that the drop front will level at about table height (30 in.) when open.

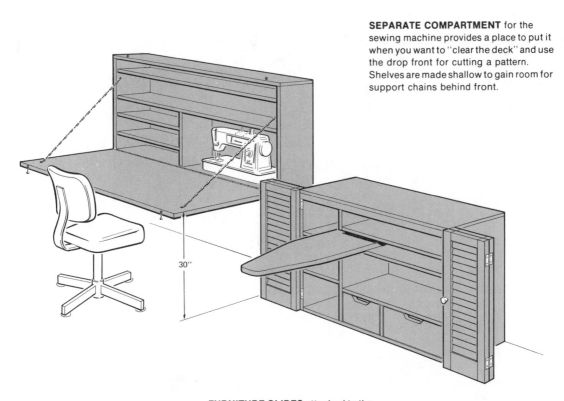

SEPARATE COMPARTMENT for the sewing machine provides a place to put it when you want to "clear the deck" and use the drop front for cutting a pattern. Shelves are made shallow to gain room for support chains behind front.

30"

FURNITURE GLIDES attached to the four corners will raise the cabinet enough to provide clearance for the louver doors.

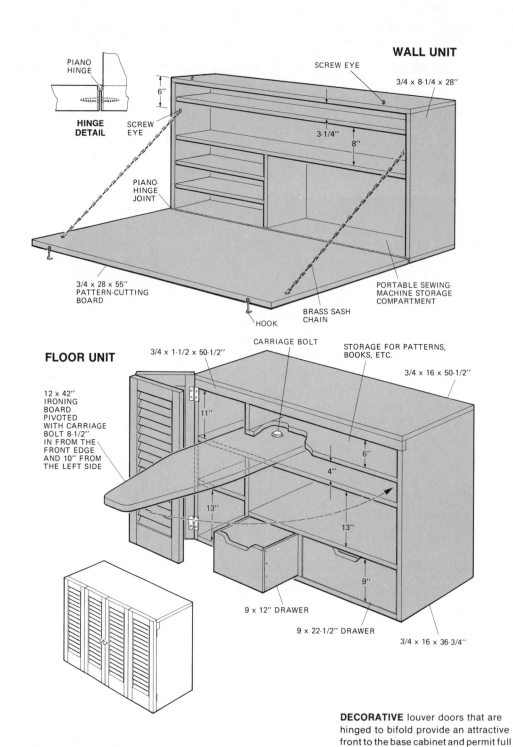

PIANO HINGE

HINGE DETAIL

SCREW EYE

6"

WALL UNIT

SCREW EYE

3/4 x 8-1/4 x 28"

3-1/4"

8"

PIANO-HINGE JOINT

3/4 x 28 x 55" PATTERN-CUTTING BOARD

HOOK

BRASS SASH CHAIN

PORTABLE SEWING-MACHINE STORAGE COMPARTMENT

FLOOR UNIT

3/4 x 1-1/2 x 50-1/2"

CARRIAGE BOLT

STORAGE FOR PATTERNS, BOOKS, ETC.

3/4 x 16 x 50-1/2"

12 x 42" IRONING BOARD PIVOTED WITH CARRIAGE BOLT 8-1/2" IN FROM THE FRONT EDGE AND 10" FROM THE LEFT SIDE

11"

6"

4"

13"

13"

9"

9 x 12" DRAWER

9 x 22-1/2" DRAWER

3/4 x 16 x 36-3/4"

DECORATIVE louver doors that are hinged to bifold provide an attractive front to the base cabinet and permit full access when open.

THIS SEWING CENTER, when open, extends to a king-size, 20x65-in. work counter. When swung up out of the way it is cleverly hidden behind a decorative wall plaque of your choice.

THE DUAL ROLE UNIT

Where space is limited and there just isn't room to have a sewing center in the way all the time, this one retracts against the wall to serve as a decorative plaque. When stored, it projects only 14 in. from the wall, leaving free floor space under it. Even when the sewing center is re-

tracted you still can get at thread and other small items.

There are three parts: a cabinet bolted securely to a wall, a counter and cutting board hinged to the cabinet, and a swing-down cabinet-leg hinged to the outboard end of the

cutting board for support. The leg has a picture-frame door that swings open to support a flip-over extension. When fully open, the cutting board measures some 65 in. long and 24 in. wide. The wall cabinet provides storage for the machine, and shelves above for sewing, patterns and what not. The cabinet-leg has shelves for odds and ends, and the back of the door has four handy trays for thread, buttons, thimbles and the like. The door front is made to look like a framed picture. Hooks and eyes keep the whole thing stored against the wall. When in use, the sewing machine is flush in a cutout in the cutting board.

Except for the two mounting cleats, the back of the wall cabinet is open. Each side is 9 x 32½ in. and is rabbeted top and bottom for 8 and 9-in.-wide members 19¼ in. long. Two 8-in.-wide shelves fit between in dadoes, the bottom one being placed 17 in. down from the top and even with the notched cutback.

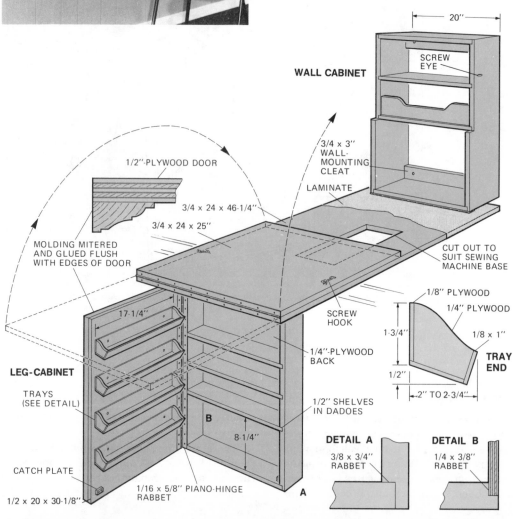

The cabinet-leg, 20 in. wide and 30¼ in. high, is made from 1x4 pine. Edges are rabbeted for a ¼-in. plywood back, side members are dadoed for ½-in. shelves, and 19¼-in. top and bottom members are housed in ⅜-in.-deep rabbets. The ½-in. plywood-panel door has a mitered frame of lumberyard molding glued to the front. Mat and picture are framed by simply gluing them to the plywood with rubber cement. Choose a painting or photograph which will look best if it is standing out a distance from the wall.

The framed door is attached with a piano hinge set in ¹⁄₁₆-in.-deep rabbets in both door and cabinet so there is no gap between the two when closed. The four spool trays vary in depth from 2 to 2¾ in., with bottom tray being the deepest. Ends are cut from ¼-in. wood, the rest from ⅛

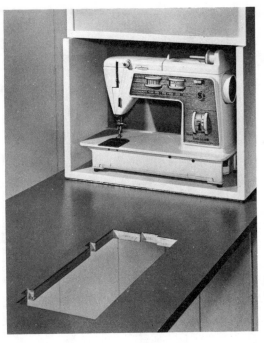

SEWING MACHINE stows in base of open wall-hung cabinet when the sewer calls it a day and closes up shop.

3/4 x 3" WALL-MOUNTING CLEAT

8"

LEG CABINET IN RAISED POSITION

7-1/4"

17"

32-1/4"

9"

PIANO HINGE

PICTURE-FRAME DOOR SUPPORTS EXTENSION LEAF

FLIP-OVER LEAF

7-1/2"

PIANO HINGE

PIANO HINGE

1/4" PLYWOOD BACK

5-1/2"

25"

46-1/4"

65-1/4"

WALL

30-1/4"

PIANO HINGE

LEG CABINET

31"

SIDE VIEW

20"

3-1/2"

MAGNETIC CATCH

FLOOR

FURNITURE GLIDES

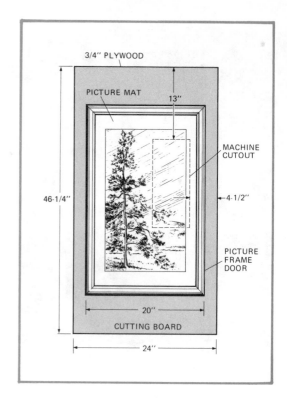

HINGED PICTURE FRAME provides access to thread and other items, even when the sewing center is stored.

in. Each tray is fastened to the door, after painting, with small oval-head wood screws.

We banded the edges of the cutting board first with plastic laminate, then covered the top surface, before hinging the extension to the end with a 20-in. piano hinge. To assure that the extension aligns properly with the cutting board when it

lies back on top of it, hold them with two C-clamps while you hinge them together. As shown in side-view drawing, the hinge point for the cabinet-leg at the outboard end of the cutting board is 7½ in. It's hinged to the wall cabinet 5½ in. from the end. Paint the cabinet to complement the decor of the room.

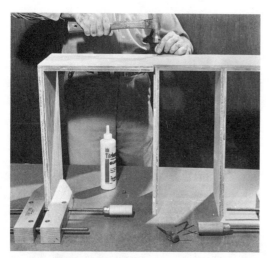

PAIR OF WOOD clamps is of great help for holding part of the wall cabinet during the first phase of assembly.

FLIP-OVER EXTENSION should align with edges of cutting board when it lies back on top for storage.

Spool cabinet

■ THE SEWER in your family will appreciate this wall cabinet for storing an easy-to-reach lineup of spools and bobbins. An 11x14-in. wooden picture frame, either purchased or made of molding, gives the project an attractive custom-cabinet look.

Edge-glue pieces for the front panel. Cut bevels to create the raised panel. Cut spool holders and bore holes for dowel pegs using jig. Cut parts (A, B, C), bore bobbin peg holes and assemble. Stain and finish with varnish.

MATERIALS LIST—SEWING CABINET

Key	Pcs.	Size and description (use)
A	2	¾ × 5 × 16½" basswood (side)
B	2	¾ × 5 × 12-⅞" basswood (top/bottom)
C	1	⅛ × 12-⅞ × 15-¾" plywood (back)
D	8	¾ × ⅝ × 9-⅞" basswood (front spool bar)
E	1	¾ × 11 × 14" basswood, two pieces edge-glued (front)
F	1	1-½ × 11 × 14" i.d. basswood (frame) with 1-¾"-wide members
G	158	³⁄₁₆"-dia. × 1-¼" dowel (pegs)
H	8	¾ × ⅝ × 11-¼" basswood (back spool bar)

Misc.: 6, 1-¼" turn buttons; pr. 1-½" brass-plated cabinet hinges; 2 sawtooth picture hangers; magnetic door catch; 2d finishing nails. glue; light walnut or other stain, varnish.

HANDSOME wall-hung cabinet is built around an 11 x 14-in. picture frame. It holds 128 spools of thread, smallest on door. 60 bobbins are stored two to a peg along bottom. Jig (right) helps you bore holes perpendicular to face of the spool bar.

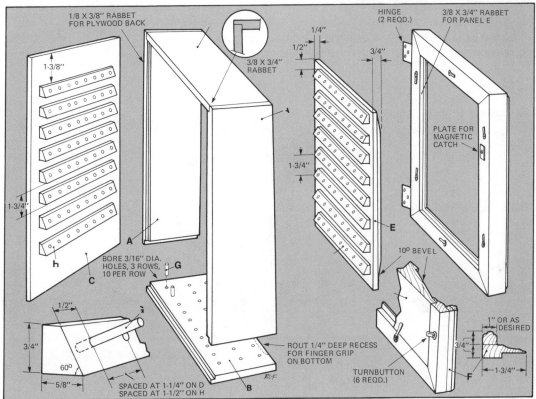

Chairside sewing cabinet

■ IF YOU LIKE TO SEW, you will love the convenience of this chairside companion. Made with ready-made legs of your choice and hardwood or hardwood-faced plywood, it is a beautiful project.

While it will necessitate gluing up boards, you'll have a more handsome piece if you build it of solid stock—walnut, birch or cherry. Not only will you be able to shape the top and bottom edges as indicated, but you'll have no problem in finishing all edges. However, if you skip the shaping of the edges of the top and bottom members and leave them square, you can use hardwood-faced plywood and cover the exposed wood with glue-on-flexible wood tape.

Start with the two inner side members. These are alike but are made right and left-hand when you're running the dadoes on the inside for the two $^3/_{16}$-in. drawer shelves. Notice that the $^1/_4$-in.-deep dadoes are stopped 1¼ in. from the front edges and then finished up by hand with a narrow chisel. If they're made with a router, you won't have to chisel them. Cut the upper dado 3 in. down from the top.

The back is the same height as the sides and is simply a plain, square-edge member. Before it can be nailed and glued to the sides, the two

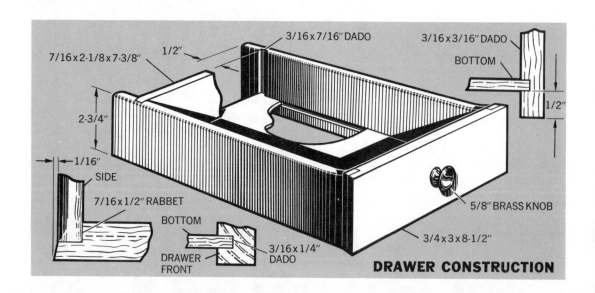

7/16 x 2-1/8 x 7-3/8"
1/2"
3/16 x 7/16" DADO
3/16 x 3/16" DADO
BOTTOM
2-3/4"
1/16"
SIDE
7/16 x 1/2" RABBET
BOTTOM
DRAWER FRONT
3/16 x 1/4" DADO
1/2"
5/8" BRASS KNOB
3/4 x 3 x 8-1/2"

DRAWER CONSTRUCTION

WITHIN ITS THREE roomy drawers and swing-out spool racks, this handy cabinet will keep all sewing essentials in one convenient place.

drawer shelves must be in place. Notice that the back member projects 1½ in. past the sides.

After gluing up stock to a width of 15½ in. cut the top and bottom members 16 in. long. They're shaped only along three sides, not the back. You'll notice that spring-loaded bullet catches are used to "lock" the swing-out spool doors, and you'll be smart if you bore the ¼-in. holes for them before you add the top and bottom members. The latter are kept flush with the back when you glue them.

Both side doors are alike but, again, they must be made right- and left-hand. The narrow fronts are joined to the sides with a miter-and-spline corner joint, after which three shelves, bored for rows of ⅛-in. dowels, are added. The upper

shelf is located 1¾ in. down from the top and the lower one is positioned ⅛ in. up from the bottom. Each door is hinged to the back (see detail). Hinge them for ¹/₁₆-in. clearance top and bottom.

The detail shows how each drawer is made. You should actually fit them to their openings, leaving enough clearance all around for free sliding. The fronts are ¾-in. stock; sides and backs are ⅜-in. The fronts are also ⅛ in. higher than the sides to lap and conceal the drawer shelves. Notice that rabbeted ends of the drawer fronts have a slight inward bevel. This assures ample side clearance for the drawer itself without a sloppy fitting front. Notice, too, that the drawers set back in ¼ in. A thumbtack at each front corner of the lower opening will keep the bottom

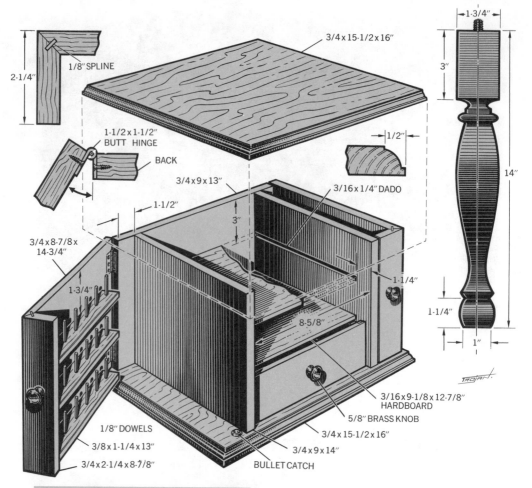

1/8" SPLINE

2-1/4"

3/4 x 15-1/2 x 16"

1-1/2 x 1-1/2"
BUTT HINGE

BACK

3/4 x 9 x 13"

1/2"

3/16 x 1/4" DADO

1-3/4"

3"

14"

1"

1-1/2"

3/4 x 8-7/8 x
14-3/4"

1-3/4"

3"

1-1/4"

1-1/4"

8-5/8"

1/8" DOWELS

3/8 x 1-1/4 x 13"

3/4 x 2-1/4 x 8-7/8"

3/16 x 9-1/8 x 12-7/8"
HARDBOARD

5/8" BRASS KNOB

3/4 x 15-1/2 x 16"

3/4 x 9 x 14"

BULLET CATCH

TROJAN

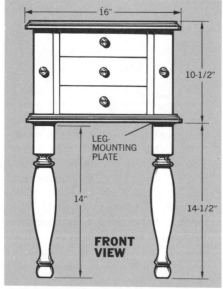

16"

10-1/2"

LEG-
MOUNTING
PLATE

14"

14-1/2"

**FRONT
VIEW**

drawer from rubbing on the cabinet and marring its finish.

If you own a router or shaper, you can give the drawers a factory-made look by rounding the top edges of the side members. You would do this, of course, before the drawers are assembled and stop the cutter at a point where the side enters the rabbet. Your cabinet is completed when you add small brass knobs.

Keep cutting edges sharp

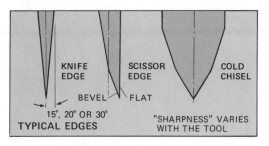

The how and why of sharpening

It won't take you long to discover that you'll get twofold benefits from keeping all cutting edges of your various tools sharp. First, your skills with chisels, knives, gouges and the like will increase because you will have better control over the tool. Second, since a dull cutting tool is far more dangerous to work with than a sharp one, you'll minimize the chance of unfortunate accidents. (A dull chisel, for example, forces *you* to do the work that the tool should be doing, by applying extra pressure.)

Though most beginning workshoppers believe that efficient sharpening is beyond their skills, the opposite is true. You can obtain, and keep, a sharp cutting edge rather than be forced to work with a ragged one—if you follow the basics listed on these pages.

Two sharpening rules of thumb you should always keep in mind:

● *Sharpen cutting tools regularly;* don't wait until they are dull and nicked because the cutting edge will then have to be reshaped on the grinding wheel.

● *Maintain the tool's original cutting-edge shape* (see examples above) *when sharpening.* Various tools call for specific degrees of bevel and shape: These shapes (degree of bevel) have proven to be the best for the particular job for which the tool is intended.

Any cutting tool that has been abused—lost its shape or nicked in its cutting edge—requires two steps for reconditioning: reshaping and sharpening. The reshaping may be done on a grinder, or with files if the tool is "soft" enough (of low carbon steel). To reshape, use coarse grit grinding stones or files. The object of reshaping is to true a tool's edge, restore proper bevels and remove all nicks. Sharpness is *not* obtained with the coarser grits. Sharpening differs from reshaping in that only the edge requires work—removal of small particles of metal to achieve a razor edge.

Grinding and grinding wheels

There are two principal types of grinding wheels: natural and man-made. The first are of fine grit and are used in water at relatively low speeds for sharpening and fine honing. To re-shape an edge, switch to one of the man-made stones (available in fine, medium-fine, medium-coarse and, occasionally, in coarse). Though several types are made, best for all-around use are long-wearing bonded and vitrified aluminum-oxide abrasive wheels. Grinding generates heat; stop frequently and water-cool the tool so its temper is not drawn. If tool becomes bluish, it's too hot and has lost its hardness. After frequent use,

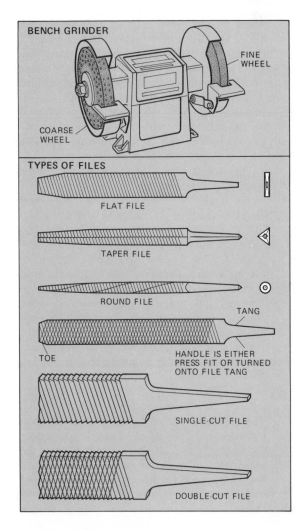

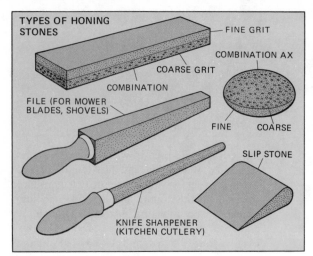

TYPES OF HONING STONES — FINE GRIT — COARSE GRIT — COMBINATION — COMBINATION AX — FINE — COARSE — FILE (FOR MOWER BLADES, SHOVELS) — SLIP STONE — KNIFE SHARPENER (KITCHEN CUTLERY)

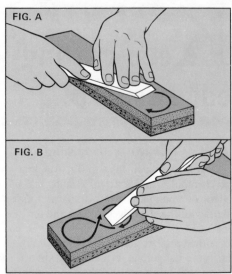

FIG. A

FIG. B

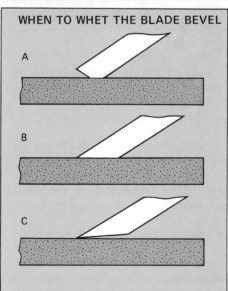

WHEN TO WHET THE BLADE BEVEL

A

B

C

metal particles may fill (load) the stone's pores. To dress a stone, use a steel wheel dresser; to dress natural stones, use a stone or a chunk of concrete.

How-tos of honing

Like grinding wheels (natural and man-made), stones must be lubricated during use, either with water or a couple of drops of fine-grade machine oil. The lubricating agent is a matter of personal preference, but most pros prefer to use oil. Oil-stones are probably the most commonly used honing stone; these are flat and may be of one grit throughout, but the combination type (see drawing above) is more practical to own.

The idea of honing is to feather the cutting edge as fine as possible. To do it, alternately stroke each side with progressively lighter pressure and finer grit abrasive. It is important that every stroke be delivered in the right direction and at the right pressure. Once you have achieved a feather edge, stop. Additional honing can be, in fact, damaging because there is good chance that you will change the tool's edge shape. The tool will be sharpened properly if, when passed lightly across your thumbnail, its edge delicately removes a scant amount of nail.

Honing stones should also be redressed occasionally and stored in a covered box.

Using files

Low-carbon cutting edges can be reshaped and sharpened with one of the files shown. The bottom edge of the cutter bar on a reel-type mower, for example, can be touched up using a flat metal-cutting file. (*Never* attempt to sharpen the reel blades unless you have the special equipment such sharpening requires.) When using files to sharpen a plane iron or chisel, support tool in

vise so bevel edge is horizontal and cutting edge is facing away from you. File toward the edge. For straight-edge chisels, use mill files; for gouges, round files. Follow filing with a honing.

Honing a chisel

To stone an edge without rounding it, use one hand to control the angle and the other to apply uniform downward pressure. In Fig. A above, burrs are removed using a circular motion. To hone bevel edge (Fig. B), keep wrists rigid and move the blade in a *continuous* figure-8 pattern. To maintain an edge which is started right, it must be occasionally whetted. In A (below), the blade needs attention all around; bevel must be taken all the way down as in B and then feathered to a razor edge as shown in C.

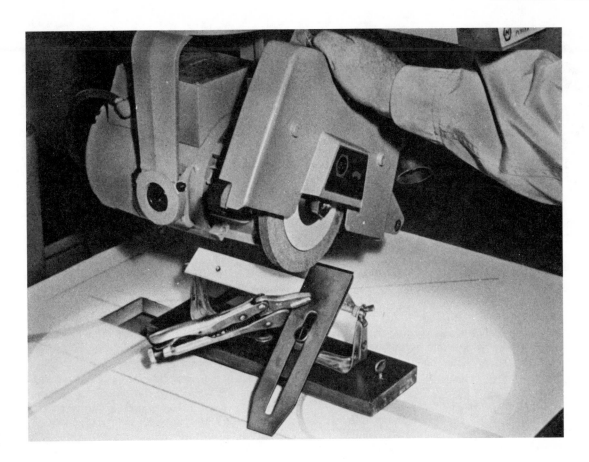

Sharpen tools on your radial-arm saw

■ TAKE FULL ADVANTAGE of your versatile radial-arm saw by adding this simple fixture that converts the saw to a precision sharpening machine.

With it, you'll be able to sharpen precisely just about any tool around your home, shop or garden, including hollow-ground chisels, plane irons, jointer and planer knives, wood bits, hedge trimmers, tin snips and other cutting tools.

The threaded studs welded to the angle iron are headless ¼-20 bolts 2 in. long, with about ½ in. of the threaded portions protruding at each end of the angle iron.

To insure alignment of the bolts with each other and with the holes in the shelf brackets, lay a section of ¾-in. angle on the inside of the 1¼-in. angle and position the bolts on the step formed by the smaller angle. Clamp the two pieces in place and tack-weld the bolts to the 1¼-in. angle. Remove the length of ¾-in. angle and complete the welding.

If necessary, enlarge the holes in the shelf brackets by reaming or drilling, then mount them on the bed of ¾-in. plywood. Note that two ¼-in. washers are placed under the bracket at the end of the bed fitted with the length of ¾-in. dowel. At the other end of the bed, a ¼-20 thumb-screw and Teenut are used to permit adjustment of the bed for slight angles or bevels.

The magnetic toolrest assembly consists of a 1-in. horseshoe magnet fitted to a 2½-in. length of ⅛ x ¾-in. flat iron. For light sharpening operations, the work can be held by the magnet

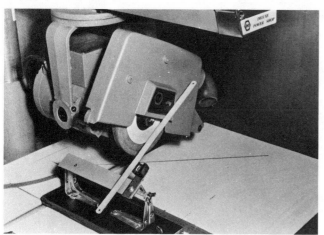

CORRECT POSITION of the angle iron is indicated when hacksaw blade falls slightly below the wheel arbor.

WING-TYPE wood bits are among many precision-ground tools you can resharpen quickly and accurately.

alone, but for heavier sharpening chores, be sure to clamp the work firmly to the angle iron.

A 100-grit, 6-in.-dia. emery wheel is used on the radial saw. Because the sharpening is always done under the wheel, you can see exactly what you're doing, especially since there is no tool-rest, wheel guard or motor housing in the way.

To get the proper plane for sharpening, lay a straightedge, such as a hacksaw blade, on the magnet and adjust the angle iron so the straightedge is slightly below the wheel arbor. Lock in this position. This procedure also provides the correct relief clearance.

Occasionally you'll find it necessary to dress the emery wheel precisely, using a diamond-tipped wheel dresser. Lock the dresser to the angle iron and position it so that it is at a "drag" position in relation to the wheel's rotation. This will also prevent the dresser from gouging pieces out of the wheel.

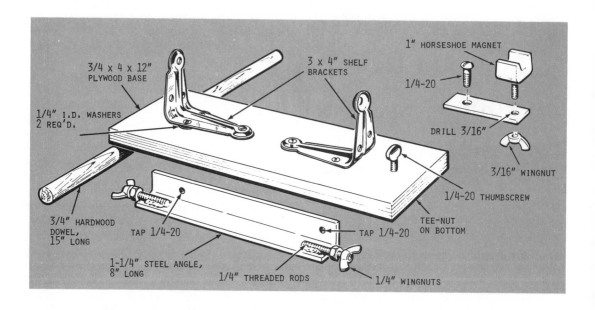

Sharpen twist drills

■ IT TAKES a pro just a few deft strokes on a grinding wheel to sharpen a twist drill, but his know-how just didn't happen. He, too, was once told the importance of maintaining equal lips.

This is the cardinal rule to follow when grinding a twist drill, since it's the perfectness of the lips that determines the roundness of the hole.

Upon examining a new drill you will note the angle is rather blunt. This is fine for drilling hard materials like alloy steels, but it doesn't work as well when drilling soft materials like aluminum, brass and plastics. The standard blunt end just doesn't work for all materials. Here is where it's worthwhile to know how to alter the original shape to produce clean, burrless holes in any material.

While lip clearance is not critical, and the angle can be anywhere from 5° to 15°, the degree of angle *must* be the same on each side. If you have normal vision, it's fairly easy to see when the lips are even, but it's still good practice to check them with a drill scale. If you find one side has been ground lower than the other, take a little off the high side.

It takes practice and a certain deftness to do this freehand. First you hold the drill with both hands, as in the photo on the next page, and gently touch the lip of the drill to the flat of the wheel. At the same time you give the drill an upward sweep with a rotating motion as shown in the drawing. Do this several times to each side while holding the drill at a 15 to 30° angle. Dip

FIVE VARYING DRILL SHAPES, left to right, are the normal, wingtip, masonry, recessed, and flat. Each is ground to suit the material.

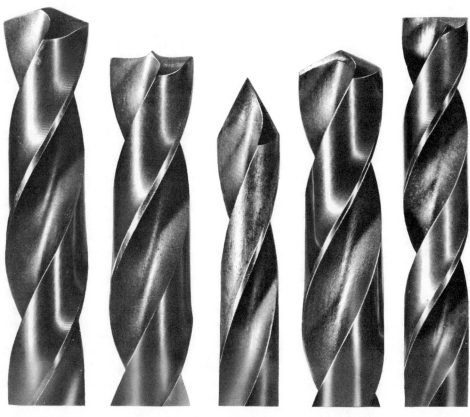

THE DRAWING and photo illustrate the proper way to hold and grind a shape best for steel.

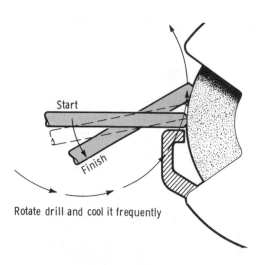

Start

Finish

Rotate drill and cool it frequently

the tip in water or oil occasionally so it doesn't overheat and turn blue. You'll wind up with an extremely sharp cutting edge which will go through the toughest of materials, including stainless steel.

To drill soft materials you need a bit which has the same lip clearance as for steel but a recess ground on the face of the lip. The recess prevents sudden catching of the drill in the work—which often results in breakage—and produces a clean, burrless hole upon breakthrough. To grind the recess, you hold the drill vertically at a 45° angle with the point down as shown in the upper left-hand photo on the next page. Then, with just slight pressure against the edge of the wheel, let the contour of the lip be your guide in a forward motion. As before, it is important to grind both sides so that they will be equally recessed.

A most versatile shape is the wingtip which produces a perfect burrless hole in the thinnest metals. The point acts much like the screw point on an auger bit in locating itself on a centerpunch mark. To grind a wingtip on a bit, place the lip at the right-hand edge of the wheel. Hold it at an opposite 5° angle and follow the same upward motion as used before.

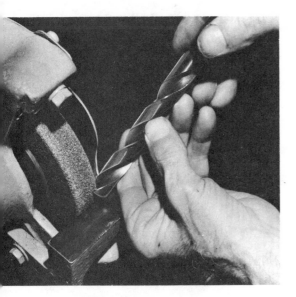

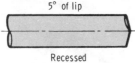

5° of lip

Recessed

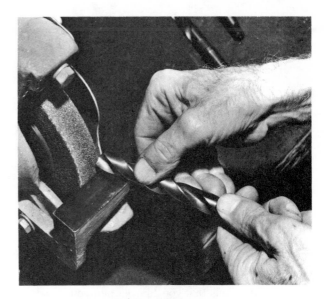

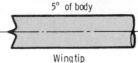

5° of body

Wingtip

TO GRIND A RECESSED LIP, hold a twist drill at the corner of the wheel with the point downward, and at a 45° angle. Touch the wheel lightly and swing the drill up.

TO GRIND A WINGTIP, place the lip against the right-hand corner of the wheel, hold at a 5° angle, and swing drill up. Do it on each side to form a point.

WHEN GRINDING a normal or masonry shape, always rotate the twist drill so it won't overheat and turn blue. Dip the end in water occasionally.

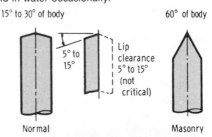

15° to 30° of body

5° to 15°

Lip clearance 5° to 15° (not critical)

Normal

60° of body

Masonry

Another shape often required is the 60° angle used for drilling masonry, plaster and tile. It's wise to use an old drill on these materials since there's a chance that you may break it, particularly when you're using the bit in a portable electric drill. To grind such a point, you simply hold the drill as before, but at a 60° angle.

By grinding both sides of the drill completely square you can make a bit which will produce a flat-bottom hole. Lip clearance is needed here, but only slightly.

The proper speed is important when drilling and should be determined by the material and the size of the twist drill. A general rule to follow is use a slow speed for hard stock and a fast speed for soft stock. The larger the drill, the slower the speed. The smaller the drill, the higher the speed. In all cases, use normal pressure. Don't force the drill, let it do the work.

When drilling a deep hole, it is good practice to withdraw the drill occasionally to free it of chips. This is particularly important when drilling aluminum and plastic. Also, when you near breakthrough in drilling, ease up on pressure and let the bit slowly sink through. You'll wind up with a neat, clean-cut hole.

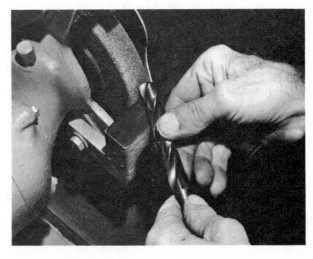

Jig to sharpen bandsaw blades

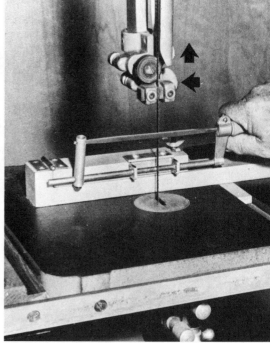

TWO-STROKE ACTION is shown by the arrows. Push forward to sharpen; pull up to position the next tooth.

■ THE UNIQUE ADVANTAGE of this sharpening jig is that you can sharpen your bandsaw blades right on the machine. It insures tooth-to-tooth spacing with such reliability that you can sharpen a 96-in.-long blade in less than 10 minutes.

The simple wooden jig for the saw table can be built quickly and easily—there are no critical dimensions, even though it will do the job with amazing precision. Use a regular bandsaw sharpening guide and simply make the brackets to hold it. These can be made of ¾-in. aluminum or steel angle. Just saw along one side of the angle and fold back the remaining flaps as indicated in the drawing. Then place the bracket on a drill press and carefully drill a pair of aligned ¼-in. holes.

Assemble the wooden portion of the jig as detailed and cut a cross member to fit into the groove on the saw table. If no miter-gauge groove is provided on your particular bandsaw, simply attach the cross member so it rides along the edge of the table. In either event, locate the cross member so that the smooth section at the end of the file will contact a tooth at the end of the first filing stroke. Then lift the handle of the file-carrying frame to bring the next tooth into position.

When initially setting up the jig, loosen the locking controls on the file-carrying frame and place the file into the space between two teeth. Then lock the controls and secure the entire jig to the table with a C-clamp. Make certain the smooth shank of the file is contacting a tooth and lift the handle until the next tooth is in the correct position. Turn down the wingnut to limit the travel of the hinged arm at this point and you're ready to begin the sharpening operation.

FORWARD MOVEMENT should stop when the tooth rests on the file's smooth shank (indicated by pencil point).

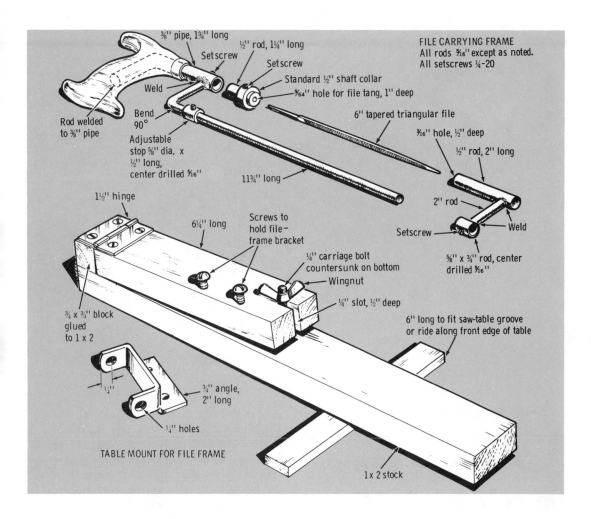

FILE CARRYING FRAME
All rods 5/16" except as noted.
All setscrews 1/4-20

3/8" pipe, 1 3/4" long

Set screw

1/2" rod, 1 1/4" long

Set screw

Weld

Rod welded to 3/8" pipe

Bend 90°

Standard 1/2" shaft collar

9/64" hole for file tang, 1" deep

6" tapered triangular file

3/16" hole, 1/2" deep

1/2" rod, 2" long

2" rod

Adjustable stop 5/8" dia. x 1/2" long, center drilled 5/16"

11 3/4" long

Weld

Setscrew

5/8" x 3/4" rod, center drilled 5/16"

1 1/2" hinge

6 1/4" long

Screws to hold file-frame bracket

1/4" carriage bolt countersunk on bottom

Wingnut

3/4 x 3/4" block glued to 1 x 2

1/4" slot, 1/2" deep

6" long to fit saw-table groove or ride along front edge of table

1/4"

3/4" angle, 2" long

1/4" holes

TABLE MOUNT FOR FILE FRAME

1 x 2 stock

ADJUST WINGNUT to stop upward movement and position the teeth. Then hold the blade lightly and sharpen.

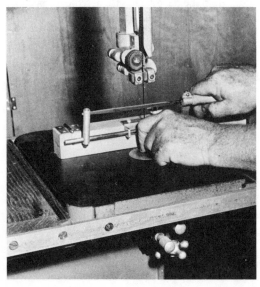

Give each tooth the same number of file strokes. Unless the saw has been badly neglected, one stroke per tooth should be sufficient.

In the event you don't use a commercial bandsaw-sharpening guide, you can make the file-carrying frame shown in the drawing. However, because the dimensions for the bracket were derived so the commercial (1/4-in. shank) tool could be used, the substitute frame will require 5/16-in. holes drilled in the bracket. Otherwise, operation and adjustments are the same.

But whether you make or buy the file-carrying frame, you're sure to appreciate the convenience of being able to quickly sharpen your bandsaw blades.

SHARPENING TOOLS is less of a chore with this unique self-oiling oilstone box. Apply steady pressure on the plunger and the pump is refilled in just a few seconds.

Oilstone can be self-lubricating

■ THE OILSTONE HOLDER shown above looks like an ordinary box used to house and protect an oilstone. Inside, it's another story. The box houses a simple pump in the base that ejects just the right amount of oil onto the stone auto-matically. The dimensions given in the drawing suit the most popular-size stone—1x2x8 in.

To make such a box, prepare a block of hardwood to the sizes given, then mark out the recesses in the base and lid to receive the stone and pump barrel. A drill press fitted with a router bit and equipped with a depth stop makes short work of removing the waste from the recesses although it can be done with a drill bit and chisel as shown at the right. Make the lid recess slightly larger than the base recess to provide an easy fit, and use a chisel to square up the corners of the recesses so that the stone will fit.

The base and lid of the box can be finished with two or three coats of polyurethane seal or shellac polish.

THE QUICKEST WAY to remove the stock from the waste portion is with a hefty bit in a drill press.

WITH MOST WASTE drilled out, a sharp chisel is used to cut a precise recess to suit your oilstone and pump.

THE BOX is rigidly clamped and the hole for the pump barrel is bored using a hand brace and bit. Be sure to keep the bit vertical.

THE PUMP BARREL is being fixed in place. Besides keeping the oil at hand, the box protects your stone from collecting dust and dirt when it's in storage.

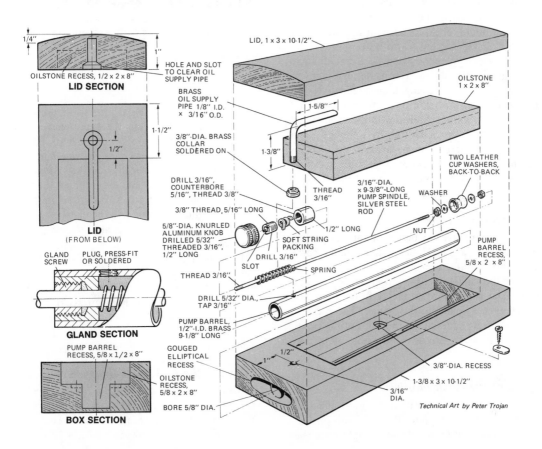

LID, 1 x 3 x 10-1/2"

1/4"
1"
OILSTONE RECESS, 1/2 x 2 x 8"
LID SECTION

HOLE AND SLOT TO CLEAR OIL SUPPLY PIPE

BRASS OIL SUPPLY PIPE 1/8" I.D. × 3/16" O.D.

OILSTONE 1 x 2 x 8"

1-5/8"

1-3/8"

1-1/2"
1/2"
LID (FROM BELOW)

3/8"-DIA. BRASS COLLAR SOLDERED ON

DRILL 3/16", COUNTERBORE 5/16", THREAD 3/8"

THREAD 3/16"

TWO LEATHER CUP WASHERS, BACK-TO-BACK

WASHER

3/16"-DIA. x 9-3/8"-LONG PUMP SPINDLE, SILVER STEEL ROD

3/8" THREAD, 5/16" LONG

1/2" LONG

NUT

GLAND SCREW
PLUG, PRESS-FIT OR SOLDERED

5/8"-DIA. KNURLED ALUMINUM KNOB DRILLED 5/32", THREADED 3/16", 1/2" LONG

SOFT STRING PACKING

DRILL 3/16"

PUMP BARREL RECESS, 5/8 x 2 x 8"

GLAND SECTION

THREAD 3/16"
SLOT

THREAD 3/16"

DRILL 5/32" DIA., TAP 3/16"

SPRING

PUMP BARREL RECESS, 5/8 x 1/2 x 8"

PUMP BARREL, 1/2"-I.D. BRASS 9-1/8" LONG

GOUGED ELLIPTICAL RECESS

1" 1/2"

OILSTONE RECESS, 5/8 x 2 x 8"

3/8"-DIA. RECESS

1-3/8 x 3 x 10-1/2"

BORE 5/8" DIA.

3/16" DIA.

BOX SECTION

Technical Art by Peter Trojan

Putting an edge on sportsman's tools

■ AN EXTRA-SHARP POINT can make all the difference in hooking a bony-mouth fish, but hooks and gaffs aren't the only edged and pointed tools essential outdoors.

A wide variety of knives, axes, hatchets and machetes also plays an important role. There are techniques you can learn to make sharpening in the outdoors easier.

No competent fishing guide or charter-boat skipper would set off without the means for re-sharpening hooks, gaffs and fileting knives. Nor would a professional hunting guide be caught in the woods without a keen blade and an imple-ment to sharpen it. Yet many anglers will fish with dull hooks, or go afield with a knife barely capable of skinning out warm butter.

And how do you chop firewood with a dull ax? With great difficulty and considerable danger. Not only are dull cutting tools ineffective, but they can bounce or skid away from the impact point. It's easy to get careless with a dull edge and try to overcome poor cutting by applying extra pressure. The result can be a nasty cut. Blades can be honed on a wheel or large stone at home, but that's not often practical afield or offshore, and hooks need special treatment.

Fish-hook sharpeners

Unquestionably, the best tool for sharpening fish hooks is a file. Hooks usually don't come from the manufacturer as sharp as they should be, and the same sometimes applies to knives and axes. The right file cuts metal faster than any stone, even a diamond-dust hone. The file also shapes cutting edges along the sides of the point, something that's almost impossible with any stone.

Types of fish-hook points

You'll get arguments about the most effective shape of a fish-hook point. Popular with profes-sional guides and knowledgeable anglers are the

STOWED IN A FISHING vest, hunting jacket or backpack, a file like this paint-scraper sharpener can be pulled out when needed to put a fast edge on fishhooks or tools.

diamond shape, triangular cut, spear point and round shape. All except the round have sharp cutting edges along the sides of the hook point to let it push its way through tough bone and carti-lage. The diamond has four cutting edges, and you can use it on all hooks except those too small to accept four cutting edges. For these hooks, it's a spear point. The round shape can be reserved for hooks so small that any shaping could weaken it.

How sharp is "sharp"? Some anglers advise the best way to test a hook is with your fingernail, not the tip of your finger. If the point isn't sharp enough to "hang" on the hard surface of the back of your nail when sliding it across with only slight pressure, then it isn't sharp enough to "hang" in-side the hard mouth of a fish.

Files are the best hook sharpeners

An ideal hook sharpener is a file designed for sharpening the tough blades of paint scrapers. You can find one at most hardware stores and occasionally in tackle shops.

Unlike other files, it's unusual in appearance—rectangular rather than tapered, 8¼ in. long by ¾ in. wide, and with both faces flat. Because it has a large tang (handle), it's easy to grip firmly and apply with lots of pressure. The fine teeth can cut anything short of an extremely hard-tempered knife blade; even on this you can touch up nicks if the knife has been properly sharpened.

Even tougher is the tiny file used for ignition points on older cars. You can carry this in a sheath glued to the underside of your fishing-pliers holster. You can also keep one in your fishing vest, with several spares in the tackle box. This file is 5¼ inches long by ⁵⁄₁₆ inch wide. Break 1½ inches off the 2¼-inch tang, leaving a ¾-inch handle. Slipping a length of small-diameter or plastic tubing over this makes a good handle.

This ignition-point file can sharpen small hooks right down to a No. 20 dry fly. Because it is designed for use on tungsten—a very hard metal—it will also smooth the toughest steel in any knife blade.

The files mentioned are ideal because they're lighter and more compact than a sharpening stone, and virtually unbreakable. They can't, however, produce quite the ultimate, even sharpness that's possible at home with a good stone. For cutting tools, the best approach is to carefully sharpen all tools before setting out. Then use the files to restore sharpness and smooth rough edges that have become dulled with use.

How to sharpen with a file

Because a file works best when the pressure stroke is toward the work, you must push the file forward against the sharp edge. Don't try to make a stroke using the full length of the file's cutting surface. That puts your hand too close to the cutting edge of the knife or ax. Unlike sharpening a hook, apply pressure during the forward stroke only. Dragging the file back across the

HOW SHARP? Slide the point of the fishhook lightly across your fingernail. If it snags, it will catch fish.

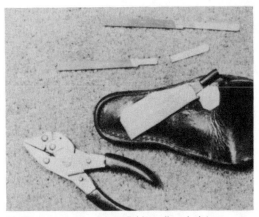

GLUE to the back of your fishing-pliers holster a small sheath to hold a tungsten ignition-point file.

FOR PUTTING a piercing point on a gaff, you may find strokes toward the tip work the best.

IN THE FIELD, with no whetstone available, the tiny ignition-point file can resharpen a knife blade.

edge you're trying to sharpen will only dull it. Lift the file off the blade completely until you're ready to start the forward pressure stroke. Apply only enough pressure to feel the file cutting the metal evenly. Too much pressure may clog the file's teeth.

Count the number of strokes and use an equal number on each side of the blade. If possible, watch an expert demonstrate sharpening at a sport show. Note the thin angle between the blade and a stone. It may appear that a back-and-forth motion is used, but actually the pressure stroke will be as the blade cuts toward the stone; pressure is relieved and the blade floats back on the return stroke.

Caring for your sharpening files

Only water is likely to damage a file seriously. If it's put away wet, rust is certain to appear in a few days; salt water can cause rust overnight. Some anglers make a simple leather sheath for their file, and keep it well oiled. You can usually get a full year's use out of a file this way.

In an emergency, you can sharpen a soft-steel

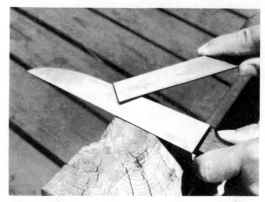

VERSATILE rectangular file sharpens knife quickly. Use short strokes to keep fingers from blade.

knife or ax somewhat with a lot of things. Try a hand-size flat rock, a brick or a chunk of concrete if nothing better is available. But for the sharpest—and safest—results, use a Carborundum or Arkansas stone for basics and pack away a file for knives and hooks afield.

EVEN A ROCK will serve as a makeshift whetstone. Using a dull knife or ax requires dangerous extra pressure.

SEVERAL popular cutting shapes for hooks are shown.

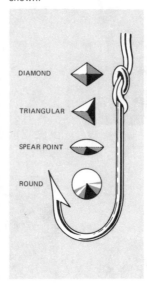

DIAMOND

TRIANGULAR

SPEAR POINT

ROUND

Wall shelves you can build

■ THE TROUBLE WITH shelves is that they collect things. You put up something originally intended for decorative glassware or a collection of beer mugs—no problem. Later, your needs change and you start loading on hefty books, hi-fi gear and that souvenir ship's anchor you found last summer. After a while, time and gravity take their toll. Suddenly your shelves fall off the wall.

Because most shelves, by their nature, will have to handle heavy loads—either now or later—it pays to get them up right the first time, especially wall-hung shelves that have no floor support. The job needn't be difficult. Commercial shelf hardware comes in types and styles to suit any need. Mounting fasteners are available for any wall surface you're likely to encounter. It's just a matter of choosing the right system.

THE ADVANTAGE of a homebuilt unit is that it can be tailor-made to provide exactly the storage you need. Such a unit is shown above. See the drawing on the next page for construction details.

ADJUSTABLE WOOD SHELVING mounted on slotted wall standards is easy to put up anywhere and permits a wide variety of attractive arrangements. As your storage needs change you can change spacing.

METAL UTILITY shelving now is available in decorator colors, and has moved into upstairs rooms.

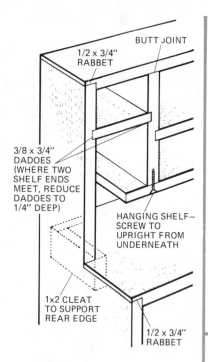

1/2 x 3/4" RABBET

BUTT JOINT

3/8 x 3/4" DADOES (WHERE TWO SHELF ENDS MEET, REDUCE DADOES TO 1/4" DEEP)

HANGING SHELF—SCREW TO UPRIGHT FROM UNDERNEATH

1x2 CLEAT TO SUPPORT REAR EDGE

1/2 x 3/4" RABBET

BASIC JOINERY is used in self-supporting shelves. Assemble joints with glue and finishing nails.

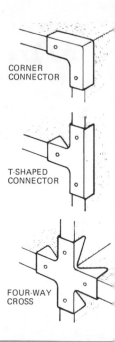

CORNER CONNECTOR

T-SHAPED CONNECTOR

FOUR-WAY CROSS

CLIP-TOGETHER ORGANIZERS

You can design your own bookcase or closet organizer with these versatile shelf connectors. The metal, tack-on clips fit standard ¾-in.-thick, prefinished shelf boards and come in corner, tee and four-way-cross styles. By combining the connectors in various arrangements, you can create compartmented storage units to suit any space and need.

VERSATILE STORAGE WALL

Perforated hardboard provides flexible storage for changing needs, can support shelf brackets as well as many special fixtures that simply hook into pre-punched holes spaced 1 in. apart. Mount panels on ⅜-in. spacers to give clearance in back for the fixture hooks (drawing below). You can also use plastic wall anchors that come with standoff collars, made especially for this purpose. Installation at right features attractive "shadow box" frame around it, with fluorescent fixtures recessed into cove at the top to give soft, indirect lighting.

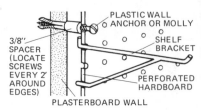

PLASTIC WALL ANCHOR OR MOLLY

SHELF BRACKET

3/8" SPACER (LOCATE SCREWS EVERY 2' AROUND EDGES)

PERFORATED HARDBOARD

PLASTERBOARD WALL

When you put up wall-hung shelves you face two basic considerations: proper wall attachment to support the total load, and proper bracket spacing to prevent the sagging of individual shelves.

For example, assuming that screws are driven into solid wood, a ¾-in. pine shelf on brackets spaced 12 in. apart will support a whopping 670 lbs. per sq. ft. But the same board on brackets 36 in. apart will hold only 38 lbs. per sq. ft.—and at 72 in., just 5 lbs.

In general, the maximum safe span for a heavily loaded ¾-in. wood shelf, with no support at the back edge, should not exceed 32 in. (Shelves in enclosed bookcases with back support can span up to 48 in.) Glass shelves of ¼-in. plate, such as typically used in medicine cabinets, should not exceed about 20 in. between the supports, though much heftier ⅜-in. plate can safely span up to 40 in.

Screws turned into thin wood paneling or plasterboard will soon pull loose. Wherever possible, it's best to screw shelf brackets into wall studs. This way, the studs—not the surface wall—support the load and no special anchors are needed.

Since studs are spaced on 16-in. centers, you can screw into every other one and maintain a sturdy 32-in. spacing. For lightly loaded shelves, or shelves of ¾ or two-by stock, you can go to every third stud.

But studs are often hard to find or may not fall exactly where you want your shelf brackets. Here you need anchors made especially for hollow walls. Screws turned into simple plastic sleeves will support hundreds of pounds and stay put indefinitely. Other types of anchors are made for solid masonry walls.

Once relegated to the basement, steel utility shelving now comes in bright, attractive decorator colors, making it equally at home in a family room, den, pantry, home office, children's room and other upstairs areas.

Consisting of predrilled angle-iron legs and lipped metal shelves, these handy bolt-together units can be assembled in minutes with only a screwdriver. They provide quick, flexible storage wherever substantial shelving is required. The leg angles have rows of closely spaced bolt holes so the height of the shelves can be adjusted easily.

Most metal utility shelving is designed to be free-standing, making it readily movable. Some units, however, can be wall-hung with special clips. Stock sizes range from 47 in. high by 30 in. wide up to 71 in. high by 42 in. wide. Shelves come 9 to 24 in. deep. For storing preserve jars and other breakables, the shelves can be mounted lip side up to keep such items from sliding off.

Homemade shelving

You can make your own utility shelving, using commercial brackets that take wood planks or big plywood sheets. Such hardware is especially handy for custom-tailoring large or odd-shaped shelves to fit a particular space, such as in attic eaves, under a stairway or over the hood of a car in a garage. Particleboard, available in sheets or in standard shelf widths, is cheap and ideal for utility use.

In a basement, where appearance is not a consideration, you can make your own hanging shelves by bolting pairs of 2x2 or 2x4 uprights, spaced several feet apart, to ceiling joists. With cross cleats nailed to the uprights at appropriate heights, you can suspend a tier of shelves from overhead. For extra-sturdy support, extend the uprights down to the floor.

Perforated hardboard

Versatile pegboard, widely used for storing tools, sports equipment and other gear, can also serve as the basis for a flexible shelf system. Metal shelf brackets, made to hook into the prepunched holes in hardboard, are available in 4- to 8-in. lengths and can take prefinished or homemade shelving boards.

UTILITY SHELVES, RACKS
Open-work shelves and racks made of vinyl-covered welded rod have light, airy look, collect less dirt than solid surfaces and are handy for use in closets, kitchen, pantry, laundry room, workshop and garage. These come in many shapes to hold typical household supplies and are easy to mount in special snap-in wall clips (below).

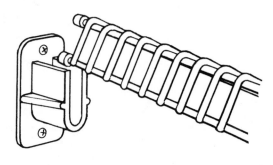

ADJUSTABLE SHELVES

When installing wall standards for adjustable shelves, care must be taken to mount all uprights at the same height so shelves will be level. Use this simple procedure: Locate first standard, mark for topmost screw and install wall anchor. Standard will hang vertically by gravity, but should also be checked for plumb with a spirit level. Mark for and install remaining anchors. Then, with first standard in place, rest a straight board and spirit level on top and mark location for top of second standard (lower left). Do the same for all succeeding standards. Check to make sure slots are at same elevation. Note in this case that standards are positioned over grooves in paneling. This avoids marring face of paneling if the shelves must be removed later.

PLASTIC SLEEVE

LEAD MASONRY SHIELD

EXPANSION BOLT (MOLLY)

COLLAPSED FOR INSERTION

EXPANDED FOR GRIP

TOGGLE BOLT

METAL UTILITY SHELVING

Metal, bolt-together shelf units are designed to be free-standing, but can also be wall-hung using special clips (right). Shelves have lipped edges that can be turned up or down. Turned up (below), the lips keep jars and other breakables from sliding off. Predrilled leg angles, available in lengths up to 6 ft., allow easy adjustment of shelves to any level.

WHICH WALL ANCHOR?

Wall-hung shelves need sturdy support. Where you can't screw into wall studs, special anchors are required to keep screws from pulling loose. For hollow walls, there are three basic types: plastic sleeve, expansion bolt (Molly) and toggle bolt. Plastic sleeve is simplest, requires only small pilot hole, is good for light to moderate loads. Mollies and toggles both work by gripping back of wall and are a better choice for heavily loaded shelves, especially deep ones that put considerable outboard strain on brackets. On solid masonry walls, you should use lead shields. These expand as lagscrews are turned into them, locking them securely in place.

INSTALLING CLOSET AND CABINET SHELVES

Installing shelves in an enclosed space, such as a closet or alcove, is easy because side walls can support the ends of shelves. Cleats of 1x2 or chair-rail stock can usually be nail-fastened to studs. Put up back cleat first, using a spirit level to ensure that it's straight (lower left). Then install end cleats, leveling them as well (bottom center). Most closets have waste space above clothes, can usually take two shelves. Where you want adjustable shelves in a cabinet or bookcase, the drawings at right show two alternate mounting methods using slotted pilaster strips or L-shaped clips that fit into rows of ¼-in. holes. (A strip of perforated hardboard makes a handy guide for locating holes 1 in. apart.)

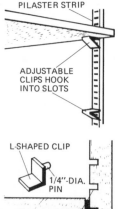

PILASTER STRIP

ADJUSTABLE CLIPS HOOK INTO SLOTS

L-SHAPED CLIP

¼"-DIA. PIN

¼"-DIA x ½"- DEEP HOLES SPACED 1" APART

BOARD SHELVES rest on rungs of ladder-like uprights, and bridge toilet to provide extra storage space.

Ladder shelves put waste space to work

ladder uprights are 1 x 2s, the rungs 1-in. dowels glued in equally spaced holes. The shelves are no deeper than the toilet tank.

■ IF YOU HAVE NEED for more storage and shelf space in your bathroom but can't see how to manage it, here's one way it can be done in most bathrooms, large or small. Make use of the wall space over the toilet. Supported by ladder-like, floor-to-ceiling uprights placed on each side of the toilet, several roomy shelves can be installed without interfering with the use of the toilet.

Even if you can't duplicate the arrangement above, in which one ladder upright supports one end of the lavatory counter and an overhead valance, a pair of uprights alone, plus two or three shelves, will provide a lot of the handy shelf space most small bathrooms sorely need. The

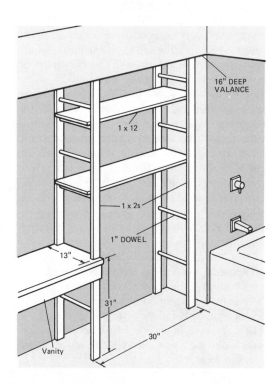

Utility shelf cover-up

SCREWS FASTENED TO CEILING JOIST

GROOVES FOR SLIDING DOORS

PERFORATED HARDBOARD

1x2 STILE

■ UTILITY SHELVING is functional but not very pretty. If you use your basement for recreation as well as storage, or if you'd just like a neater-looking garage, you want those cluttered shelves out of sight. The ones shown here were covered up inexpensively with a few sheets of prefinished ⅛-in. plywood paneling.

Panel doors slide in double grooves in kiln-dried 2x4 rails; it's important that the lumber you buy for these rails is straight. Grooves are made with a router or cut on a table saw (or you can have this step done at the lumberyard.) Shelving must be securely fastened to the wall. Fasten the rails to shelf uprights and to ceiling joists, where possible, with wood screws. The rails must be level; if shelves were made inaccurately, shims may be necessary. Vertical 1x2 end strips are fastened with glue and finishing nails. Make the framework wider than the shelves, close the sides in with perforated hardboard, and you'll have extra space for hanging storage. Panels are cut ⅜ in. shorter than the distance between bottom of lower groove and top of upper groove; cut a test strip to be sure of this dimension. Cut wide enough to allow at least 1-in. overlap between panels; bowing will be less likely if grain is vertical.

After the framework has been sanded, primed and painted (with gloss enamel for easy cleaning), bottom grooves are rubbed with beeswax to help panels slide smoothly. To dress up panel edges, glue on ⅛-in. plastic report-cover spines. These are sold in a variety of colors by office-supply outlets. Spines that will fit ¼-in. paneling are also available.

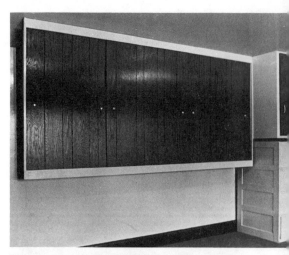

FRAMEWORK AND PANELING produce a handsome cabinet look. Recessed pulls are pressed into 1-in. holes in panels, should be above children's reach.

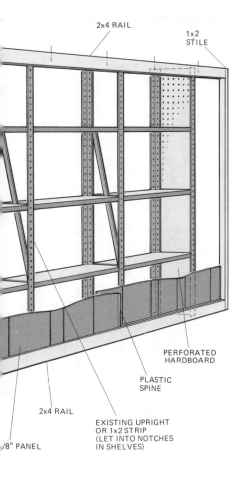

2x4 RAIL

1x2 STILE

PERFORATED HARDBOARD

PLASTIC SPINE

2x4 RAIL

EXISTING UPRIGHT OR 1x2 STRIP (LET INTO NOTCHES IN SHELVES)

/8" PANEL

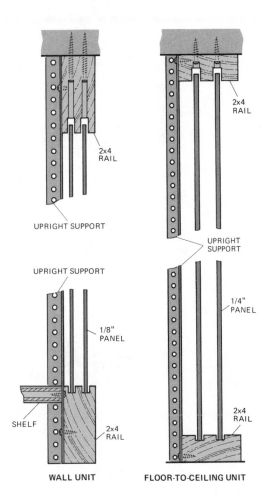

2x4 RAIL

UPRIGHT SUPPORT

UPRIGHT SUPPORT

UPRIGHT SUPPORT

1/8" PANEL

1/4" PANEL

SHELF

2x4 RAIL

2x4 RAIL

WALL UNIT

FLOOR-TO-CEILING UNIT

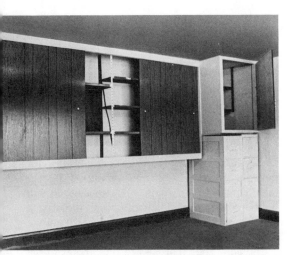

STORAGE SPACE inside is plentiful. Enclosure with a hinged door (paneling on ½-in. plywood) was made oversize for maximum space above the existing cabinet.

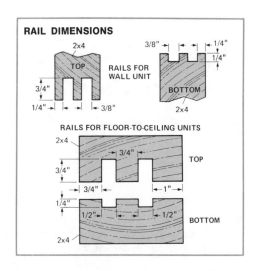

RAIL DIMENSIONS

2x4

TOP

RAILS FOR WALL UNIT

3/8"   1/4"

1/4"

3/4"

BOTTOM

1/4"   3/8"

2x4

RAILS FOR FLOOR-TO-CEILING UNITS

2x4

3/4"

3/4"

TOP

3/4"

1"

1/4"

1/2"   1/2"

BOTTOM

2x4

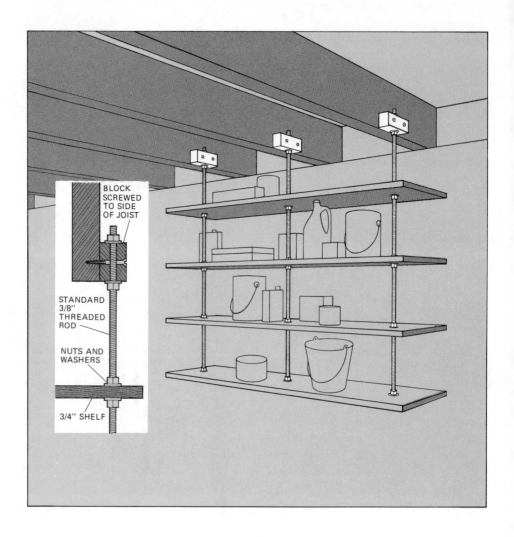

BLOCK SCREWED TO SIDE OF JOIST

STANDARD 3/8" THREADED ROD

NUTS AND WASHERS

3/4" SHELF

Put up shelves that stay up

■ SHELVES CAN MEAN the difference between order and disorder in the basement, attic or garage, and they're something you can't have too many of for holding such things as cans of leftover paint, garden sprays and insecticides, balls, mitts and bats, clippers and shears, holiday decorations, luggage, tools and boots.

There are about as many ways to support shelves as there are things to store. Shown on the facing page are six of the more common ways for installing them between end uprights or fastening them to walls or studs. All arrangements will hold a considerable load without giving way.

A novel way to hang shelves is shown above: Two or more boards are suspended from a series of threaded rods that pass through holes in the boards and wood blocks screwed to the basement joists.

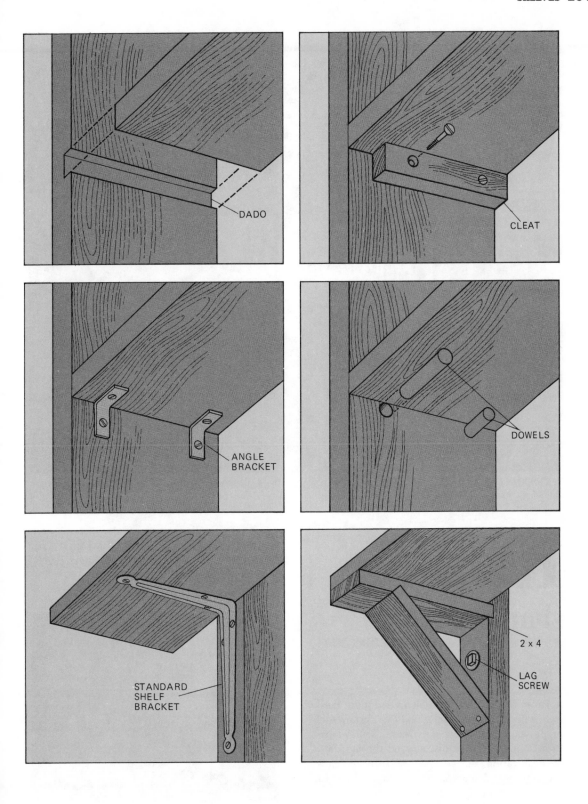

DADO

CLEAT

ANGLE BRACKET

DOWELS

STANDARD SHELF BRACKET

2 x 4

LAG SCREW

IN THIS CAREFULLY planned workshop, all of the available space is used for handy storage of tools and hardware. Good lighting is a must to do quality work.

Keep your shop organized

■ FEW WORKSHOP problems are more frustrating than being unable to find that certain tool or jig when you know it's around somewhere. Projects may even be discouraged through lack of organization. But you may be surprised how inventive organizing a workshop can be. Start by clearing everything out and cleaning up the space. You might even repaint.

After all the junk has been tossed out, lay out tools and useful materials in function-oriented groups. This will give you an idea of how much space is needed for storage of each group. Consider ways in which valuable floor space can be saved and made flexible.

GROUP TOOLS BY USE

ALL SIMILAR TOOLS (saws, clamps and wrenches) are stored in the same area. To gain work space, table saw rolls partially under radial saw.

KEEP TOOLS NEARBY

EASY ACCESS is important. Bits and accessory tools for drill press are to immediate left of machine.

INCREASE STORAGE AREAS

By reinforcing the legs of this old table with ½-in. plywood, it is stable enough to support a wood lathe and it provides more storage space in the process. You can leave yours open underneath, but if more shelving is needed, this would be ideal.

PLYWOOD SKIRT on old dining table provides storage for lathe tools. Large items are stored underneath.

DESIGN A FLOOR PLAN

FLOOR PLAN—WORKSHOP

Key	Description
A	Main workbench
B	Cupboard (portable power tools)
C	Nail, screw and bolt storage shelves
D	Grinder bench (handsaws below)
E	Table saw
F	Radial-arm saw
G	Belt and disc sander
H	Sabre saw and router table
I	Roll-out shop vacuum
J	Storage cabinet (old dishwasher)
K	Drill press
L	Lathe table
M	General storage shelves
N	Lally column
O	Tool storage wall
P	4-ft., single-tube fluorescent light
Q	4-ft., double-tube fluorescent light
R	3-ft. single-tube fluorescent light

Note: Overall garage dimensions are about 19½ × 22 ft.

MAKE LIFT OUT DOORS

Conventional doors under a workbench have drawbacks. Sliding doors leave the storage space half-closed. Conventional doors require swinging space at cabinet front. The door shown solves both problems. The 28x60-in. door is hinged at the bottom to swing open bin-fashion. When you need repeated access to the storage space, the entire door can be pulled out.

First, bore the dowel holes in a length of 2x4 to size. Bore the holes 3 in. deep and about 8 in. from the ends. Rip the 2x4 down the middle to make two pieces about 1½ in. wide by 1¾ in. thick. Keep the cut-edge sides face-to-face so dowel holes remain aligned; then attach one

piece to bench or to legs to form stationary rail. Mark and set butt hinges as shown on the other rail and doorframe rail. A ⅛x½ in.-deep groove was cut in door frame to suit panel.

MATERIALS LIST—REMOVABLE DOOR

Key	No.	Size and description (use)
A	2	1½ · approx. 1¹¹⁄₁₆ · 60″ upper and lower rails (ripped from same 2 × 4)
B	2	¾ · 2 · 60″ mitered rails
C	2	¾ · 2 · 28″ mitered stiles
D	1	⅛ · 25 · 57″ finished panel
E	1	¼ · 1 × 26″ stiffener
F	4	2½″ corner irons
G	2	2″ butt hinges
H	2	⅝ × 3″ wooden dowels
I	2	5¾″ door pulls

Misc: Carpenter's glue, fh wood screws

PULL TOP of door out slightly and lift evenly on door handles to disengage dowels. Door can be set aside for full access to storage.

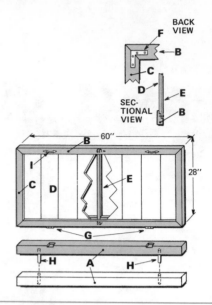

STORE ITEMS IN JARS

BABY-FOOD JARS can store nails, screws, nuts, plus assorted items. Larger bottles aligned on lower shelf hang by caps. Attach caps with centered screw and off-center brad.

As numerous shop owners discovered long ago, baby-food bottles are ideal keepers for storing all kinds of small items. Several large shelves above a workbench can accommodate over 100 of these jars. By adding a smaller shelf between, you can fit three rows and still have space left on the wider shelves for tools you want to keep nearby.

If you want to hang the larger bottles from underneath as shown, allow adequate finger clearance when attaching the caps; otherwise the jars will be difficult to loosen. Stick-on labels should be used to identify those jars with similar contents. A small utility light—like the gooseneck lamp shown—is good for sorting and selection.

COMBINE TOOL TABLES

This combination table serves two useful purposes: It keeps the router and sabre saw (used as substitute shaper and jigsaw) handy at all times and saves floor space by combining the two tools into one fold-up unit. The framework shown was originally used to hold industrial electronic equipment; it was salvaged from the local dump. Admittedly, you won't find a duplicate, but it would be easy to build a similar table from angle iron welded or bolted together, or even from wood.

The easiest way to mount the sabre saw on the top level is to use a commercial sabre-saw table that comes with saw-mounting and accessory hardware to make the tool a jigsaw. Add a wood frame around the metal saw table to custom-fit it

to the slightly larger framework.

You can also add a hold-down, spring-loaded arm as shown in the photo. By fastening a plastic pill-bottle cap over the slotted working end of the arm, you protect the sabre saw blade.

MATERIALS LIST—HOLD-DOWN ARM

Key	No.	Size and description (use)
A	1	8", 2 × 4 vertical support
B	1	3/4 × 1 1/2 × 14 1/2" arm
C	1	compression spring
D	1	3 1/2" long, 1 1/2" angle iron
E	1	1/4" machine screw
F	2	nuts
G	1	washer
H	1	dowel (spring retainer)
I	1	1/4 × 4" threaded rod
J	2	nuts
K	2	washers
L	1	pill bottle and cap

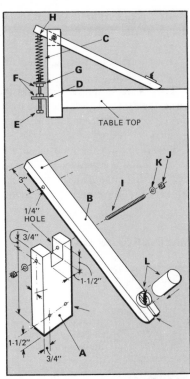

SALVAGED METAL frame provides a handy place for sabre saw table on top level, and makes the router a shaper on the lower slide-in table. Commercial saw table was adapted to the stand dimensions by adding a frame. An optional hold-down arm includes a "pill bottle" safety feature to protect the blade and your fingers.

HANG SAWS TEETH IN

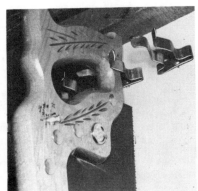

HANDSAW STORES under a narrow shelf. Clips hold larger saws; a coathanger wire is bent to grab the smaller saws. A closed loop in a piece of wire is attached to the shelf bottom with a screw eye. Saws sorted this way need less space while the blade teeth remain well protected.

Most people store their handsaws flat, and by doing so use space that is better left to other things.

You can create the storage system under an 8 x 48-in. grinder shelf.

The 2¾-in. spring clamps hold the top of my large saws securely, while the two ½-in.-thick dowels on the bottom serve to keep each blade aligned.

It works best if these dowels are loose enough to turn when the blade is inserted. Smaller saws can be hung either from wire hooks, or from finish nails that have been driven into the wall.

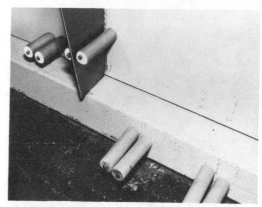

SPACED PAIR of dowels keeps the saw tips from swinging. Install them by using 8d nails.

MAKE A ROAMING VISE

ROAMING VISE uses a clamp that came from an old dough mixer. It's an easy-to-make clamp.

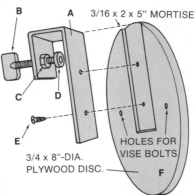

B   A   3/16 x 2 x 5" MORTISE

C   D

E

3/4 x 8"-DIA.
PLYWOOD DISC.

HOLES FOR
VISE BOLTS

F

An extra vise can be converted into a roaming vise by mounting it on a piece of ¾-in. plywood and then clamping this unit wherever it's needed. You can make your own clamp by bending flat-iron bar stock into a U-shape and welding a large nut on the lower arm to accept a wing bolt. If the vise vibrates when doing heavy work, just slip a thin wood shim between the base and the bench. When the wedge is properly fitted, the play will disappear and you can glue it to the base to make the adjustment permanent.

MATERIALS LIST—VISE

Key	No.	Size and description
A	1	3/16 × 2 × 9½" flat iron bar
B	1	4" thumbscrew
C	1	nut, welded to flat iron
D	1	collar to suit nut
E	2	¾", No. 7 fh screws
F	1	¾ × 8"-dia. plywood disc

MORE TIPS FOR GETTING MORE ENJOYMENT FROM YOUR SHOP

Try to avoid the temptation to hang a lot of tools, such as spring clamps or wrenches, from one nail. Although it may save space, the tool you want always seems nearest the wall. The space saved may cause some aggravation and usually isn't worth it.

Once your shop is organized and everything is in place, make a special effort to keep it that way. Allow time for cleanup after each work session. You will be more eager to get back to your projects—when you know everything is in order. On the other hand, if you leave the shop or project in a mess, you will be less anxious to get back to the job.

If you have youngsters, or particularly a teen-age son with an interest in your shop, keeping it orderly will encourage a tool's return to its proper place. It doesn't work like magic, but it helps.

Lumber, pipe, panels and rarely used cutting jigs are best stored high up and out of the way. Ceiling joists or collar beams are usually exposed in a garage workshop and these make instant racks for this purpose. Remember to store large items in a way that allows easy retrieval. Trying to move heavy objects about while working over your head is an easy way to injure your back.

An organized shop is a safe shop, but remember that your shop is only as safe as you are. Power tools make work more enjoyable, but they require extra attention when in use. Always keep safety glasses near your power tools as a reminder to use them.

Shop organizer

■ THIS SHOP organizer is not as tedious to make as it looks—you just need to know a couple of shortcuts. For the "drawers," you can use plastic boxes, sardine cans, tuna cans, jar lids—whatever you can collect in quantity and at low cost. Use ⅛-in. hardboard for a light-duty organizer, ¼-in. for heavy duty.

Determine strip lengths and widths according to the size and number of drawers you desire. To cut slots, clamp, drill and fasten about eight strips together with two fh bolts, washers and nuts. Countersink the bolt head if you intend to cut the slots on a stationary power saw. Lay out the slots on the top strip. You can cut the slots with a

handsaw, bandsaw, jigsaw or table saw. (The latter allows you to cut more plies per pass, but don't cut more than six plies per pass.) Use one of finished strips as a template for laying out top strip on next stack.

Test-assemble the dividers without glue, front side down on a flat surface. Remove one vertical strip at a time and coat all contact surfaces with yellow carpenter's glue. Once all strips have been glued, square up unit and allow to dry. Finally, glue on sides.

Sides can also be made of 1-in. pine for greater rigidity. To fasten sides to dividers, glue and clamp. Organizers can be used in any room.

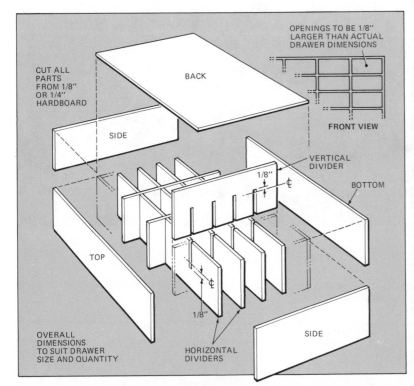

CUT ALL PARTS FROM 1/8" OR 1/4" HARDBOARD

BACK

SIDE

OPENINGS TO BE 1/8" LARGER THAN ACTUAL DRAWER DIMENSIONS

FRONT VIEW

VERTICAL DIVIDER

BOTTOM

1/8"

TOP

SIDE

OVERALL DIMENSIONS TO SUIT DRAWER SIZE AND QUANTITY

HORIZONTAL DIVIDERS

CHECK WIDTH of divider slots with scrap of hardboard prior to assembly.

APPLY GLUE to dividers and joints and assemble on a flat work surface.

Eggs hold small parts

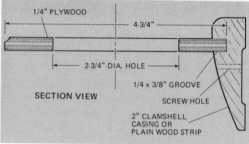

1/4" PLYWOOD

4-3/4"

2-3/4"-DIA. HOLE

1/4 x 3/8" GROOVE

SECTION VIEW

SCREW HOLE

2" CLAMSHELL CASING OR PLAIN WOOD STRIP

■ MANY THROWAWAY CONTAINERS have been put to use in the home and workshop to hold a variety of things. Baby-food jars have made great holders for screws, nails and the like. Modified bleach bottles have served a multitude of uses from grain scoops to paintbrush holders to funnels. Still another container that lends itself to holding things is the egg-shape one in which panty hose are sold. It consists of a two-part white plastic shell. The half shells provide perfect little cups for brads, screws, nails, you name it, when supported by a shelf. Being conical in shape, they make it easy to pick out the very last brad, and the upper half of the shells can serve as covers.

A row of holes 5 in. on centers is made in a scrap of plywood with a circle cutter chucked in a drill press; then the plywood is glued in a groove run in a scrap of clamshell door casing.

Tool caddy from scraps

■ REPAIR JOBS around the home often require trips back to the workshop for forgotten tools or supplies. The tool caddy here should eliminate such wasted time. It not only totes a wide assortment of tools, but also organizes fasteners and spare parts. Since the organizers are interchangeable, you can fit out the caddy for specific tasks.

Construction of the caddy is simple, but atten-

tion must be paid to the clever latches and retainers for the saws and hammer. The hammer, which also serves as the caddy handle, is held in place by pipe strapping at the handle end and by a spring-loaded latch at the neck (see detail in plans). A strap and buckle or an L-shaped steel bar installed in slots cut above the hammer's neck in the cradle will also work. The protruding end of corner brace (U) keeps the hammer from sliding forward.

A machine screw (M), brazed to the corner brace, serves as an anchor for spring F. Two chain links (G) fasten to the spring and engage the blade-tensioning bolt on a hacksaw. A similarly devised hook secures the backsaw at the other end of the caddy. Instead of chain links, a hook bent from hanger wire engages the saw handle.

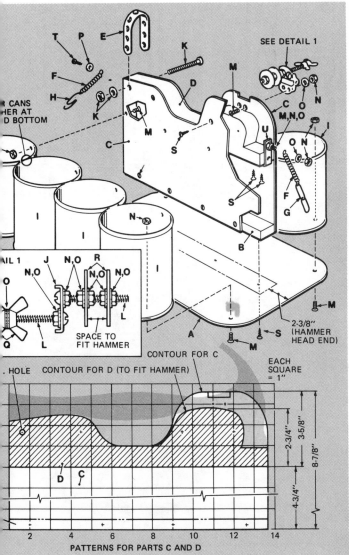

MATERIALS LIST—TOOL CADDY

Key	No.	Size and description (use)
A	1	⅛ x 9⅜ x 16¼″ hardboard (caddy base)
B	1	½ x 1 x 12⅝″ pine (saw-holder base)
C	2	⅛ x 8⅞ x 12⅝″ hardboard (saw-holder sides)
D	1	1 x 2⅜ x 12⅝″ overall (hammer cradle); sandwich ¾″ pine between 2 pieces of ⅛″ hardboard
E	1	3″ pipe strapping (handle retainer)
F	2	⅛″-dia. x 2″ spring
G	1	2-link piece of chain (to catch on hacksaw)
H	1	hook bent from stiff wire (to catch on backsaw)
I	8	4″ dia. cans
J	1	self-closing cabinet hinge
K	1	¼-20 x 1½″ machine screw, nut and washer
L	2	No. 8-32 x 1¼″ machine screw
M	15	No. 8-32 x ½″ machine screw
N	22	No. 8-32 hex nut
O	11	No. 8 external-tooth lock washer
P	1	flat washer
Q	2	No. 8-32 wingnut
R	2	1″ o.d. flat washer
S	20	⅝″ No. 8 fh screw
T	1	No. 8 pan-head screw
U	1	corner brace

Tool holders from hardware cloth

■ INEXPENSIVE SCRAPS of hardware cloth are ideal for making tool holders in a variety of shapes. The ready-made openings in the wire mesh save the work of boring holes in wood racks, and they accommodate a wide assortment of tools.

Two easily made racks are shown here: one for use on a bench and one for wall mounting.

To keep tools neatly upright, you need two levels of mesh—one at the top and one underneath to catch the tips. In the wall rack, this is accomplished by rolling an 8x9-in. piece of mesh into a 2¼-in.-diameter cylinder. This looks attractive and allows you to insert tools at various angles. The cylinder is held at the ends by wood discs glued into a U-shaped bracket. The back of the bracket extends 3 in. below the cylinder to keep the tips of slanted tools from scratching the wall.

The bench rack is just a U-shaped wood stand fitted with two levels of mesh about 1½ in. apart. Bend the edges of the mesh down at 90° all around to add stiffness. Shape the pieces first before determining final dimensions for the stand. The mesh is held in place by small bolts.

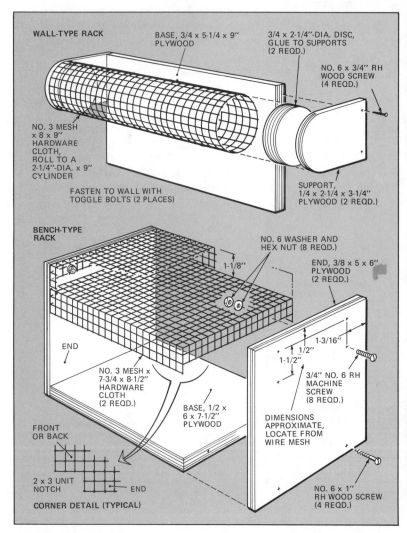

WALL-TYPE RACK

BASE, 3/4 x 5-1/4 x 9" PLYWOOD

3/4 x 2-1/4"-DIA. DISC, GLUE TO SUPPORTS (2 REQD.)

NO. 6 x 3/4" RH WOOD SCREW (4 REQD.)

NO. 3 MESH x 8 x 9" HARDWARE CLOTH, ROLL TO A 2-1/4"-DIA. x 9" CYLINDER

FASTEN TO WALL WITH TOGGLE BOLTS (2 PLACES)

SUPPORT, 1/4 x 2-1/4 x 3-1/4" PLYWOOD (2 REQD.)

BENCH-TYPE RACK

NO. 6 WASHER AND HEX NUT (8 REQD.)

1-1/8"

END, 3/8 x 5 x 6" PLYWOOD (2 REQD.)

END

NO. 3 MESH x 7-3/4 x 8-1/2" HARDWARE CLOTH (2 REQD.)

BASE, 1/2 x 6 x 7-1/2" PLYWOOD

1-3/16"
1/2"
1-1/2"

3/4" NO. 6 RH MACHINE SCREW (8 REQD.)

DIMENSIONS APPROXIMATE, LOCATE FROM WIRE MESH

FRONT OR BACK

2 x 3 UNIT NOTCH

END

CORNER DETAIL (TYPICAL)

NO. 6 x 1" RH WOOD SCREW (4 REQD.)

PORTABLE BENCH rack puts small tools within easy reach.

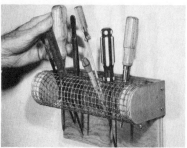

WALL RACK uses hardware cloth formed into a cylinder.

EASY WAY to shape the cylinder is to roll mesh around a caulking cartridge.

Cutting board for your shop

■ A GOOD CUTTING BOARD is a valuable tool for both shop and darkroom work. Besides giving you accurate results every time, one will keep other surfaces from being marred by routine cutting jobs.

This board can be scaled to any size that meets your needs. Rather than incorporating a knife, it allows you to use the cutting tool most appropriate for whatever job you're doing by running it along a solid metal straightedge. The adjustable stop facilitates repeated cuts. If you're left-handed, you'll find the board easy to work with, too.

Dimensions given in the drawing are for a board about as large as you can work on comfortably. If you scale it down, the press bar should still be at least 13/16 in. high and 2 in. wide, and of a good grade of hardwood. For the baseboard, use fir plywood, ¾ x 27½ x 30½ in., cut as shown. Note that the press bar and its extensions are 1 in. thick overall, while the anchor blocks are 1³/₁₆ in. thick. This allows material up to ¼ in. thick to be cut against the length of the fence. Thicker materials can be cut between the anchor blocks.

The 20-ga. sheet metal is 1 in. wide, rabbeted into the press bar so it is flush on the underside, and extends ¹/₁₆ in. beyond it. The metal is attached with contact cement; clamping is advisable for this step, and be sure there's always adequate ventilation when you're working with contact cement. The 45° cut on the press bar is made after the straightedge has been cemented in place.

The anchor blocks, attached to the baseboard with screws and glue, must be positioned accurately, since they will determine the ultimate squareness of the board. Small errors can be compensated for by shimming the hinges connecting the blocks to the press bar.

VERSATILITY of the cutting board is demonstrated by its handling of a wide variety of materials. At top, picture mats with beveled edges are readily and accurately made. The bevel of the press bar makes the cutting angle precise. The middle photo shows the board with the stop removed to permit cutting of an extra-large sheet. A roll-paper holder, shown in use in the photo allows cutting of roll materials up to 24 in. wide, including photographic paper.

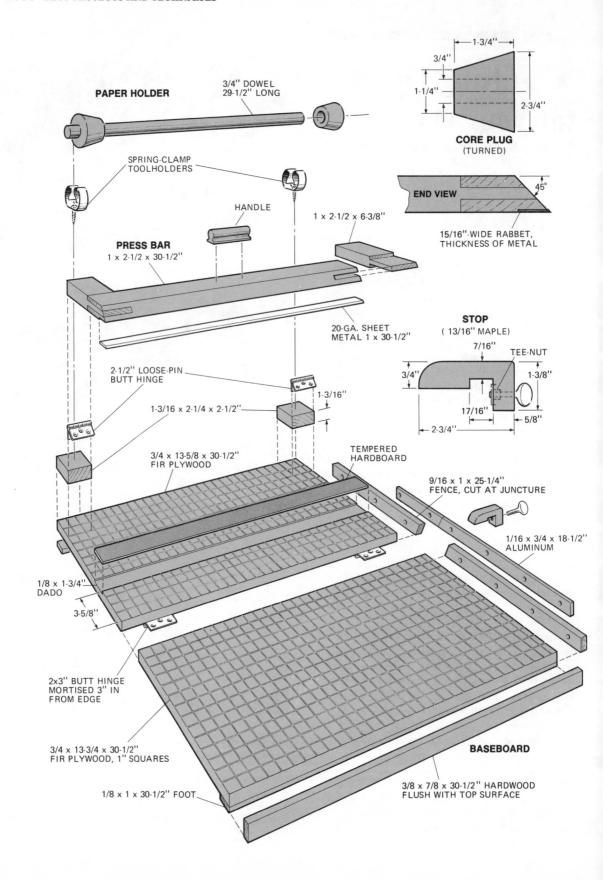

PAPER HOLDER

3/4'' DOWEL
29-1/2'' LONG

CORE PLUG
(TURNED)

1-3/4''
3/4''
1-1/4''
2-3/4''

SPRING-CLAMP
TOOLHOLDERS

HANDLE

1 x 2-1/2 x 6-3/8''

END VIEW
45°

15/16''-WIDE RABBET,
THICKNESS OF METAL

PRESS BAR
1 x 2-1/2 x 30-1/2''

20-GA. SHEET
METAL 1 x 30-1/2''

STOP
(13/16'' MAPLE)

7/16''
TEE-NUT
3/4''
1-3/8''
17/16''
5/8''
2-3/4''

2-1/2'' LOOSE-PIN
BUTT HINGE

1-3/16 x 2-1/4 x 2-1/2''

1-3/16''

3/4 x 13-5/8 x 30-1/2''
FIR PLYWOOD

TEMPERED
HARDBOARD

9/16 x 1 x 25-1/4''
FENCE, CUT AT JUNCTURE

1/16 x 3/4 x 18-1/2''
ALUMINUM

1/8 x 1-3/4''
DADO

3-5/8''

2x3'' BUTT HINGE
MORTISED 3'' IN
FROM EDGE

3/4 x 13-3/4 x 30-1/2''
FIR PLYWOOD, 1'' SQUARES

BASEBOARD

1/8 x 1 x 30-1/2'' FOOT

3/8 x 7/8 x 30-1/2'' HARDWOOD
FLUSH WITH TOP SURFACE

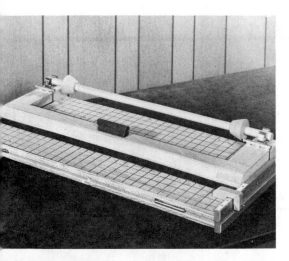

The routed or plowed ⅛ x 1¾-in. dado in the baseboard is for the replaceable tempered hardboard cutting surface, which should be cut for a snug fit. There are actually four different cutting surfaces, as the hardboard can be turned end for end, then turned over and finally turned end for end again before replacement.

The fence is secured with 1½-in. No. 10 screws, and the 1/16-in. aluminum, on which the stop rides, is attached to it with No. 4 screws. A commercially available metal tape with a pressure-sensitive adhesive back was used for the scale; a yardstick ripped to the proper width would be a suitable alternative.

Core plugs for the paper holder are turned on the lathe using the screw center and bored for ¾-in. dowel before being cut off from waste stock.

It is advisable to clamp the assembled anchor blocks and press bar to the baseboard before laying out the 1-in. squares. Measurement should start from the metal straightedge on the press bar for the lines that will be parallel to it, and from the upper edge of the baseboard or fence for the others.

Stain and finish the completed cutting board as desired. A clear resin sealer and urethane varnish were used here.

THE CUTTING BOARD FOLDS for storage (top left), but can be built more simply when space is no problem. With the folding feature omitted, the ⅛-in. feet, otherwise required by the hinge thickness, are no longer needed. In the middle photo, V-grooves are cut 1/32 in. deep with a thin saw blade set at 45°; a single pass will complete each V-cut. A molding head with V-knives could also be used. At left, grooves are darkened with a fine-point felt-tip marking pen before final finishing of the board. Paint or India ink also work.

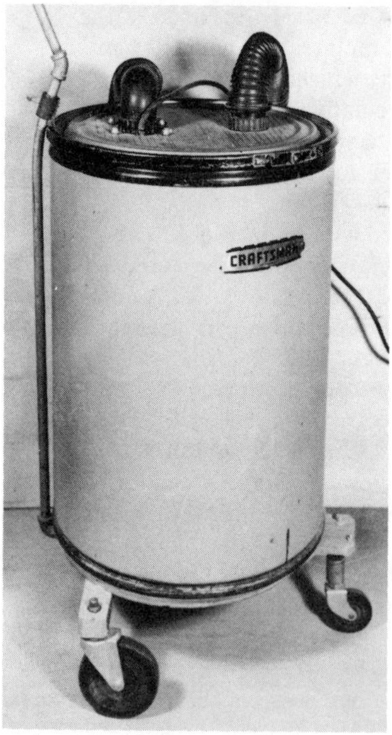
CRAFTSMAN

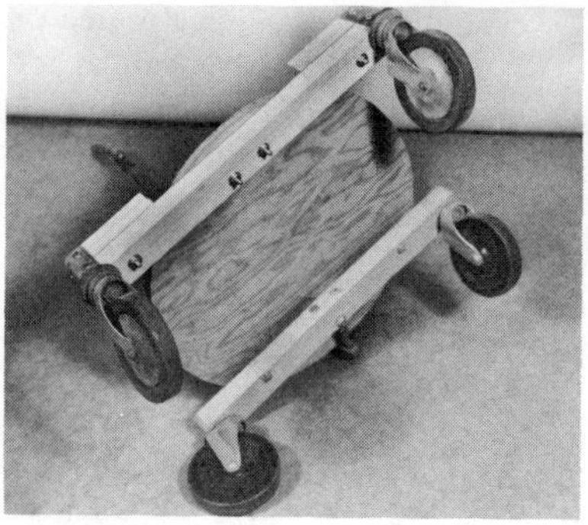

MATERIALS LIST—VACUUM DOLLY

Key	No.	Size and description (use)
A	1	¾ x 17⅝" dia. plywood (base)
B	1	¾ x 4½ x 8" pine (small caster support)
C	2	5/4 x 2 x 20½" pine** (caster support)
D	1	¾" IPT x 3" dia. stem-type caster*
E	1	¾" IPT connector*
F	1	¾" IPT nipple*
G	1	¾" IPT floor flange*
H	3	¼-20 x 1½" machine screw, nut, washer*
I	3	¼-20 x 2" machine screw, nut and washer*
J	2	5/4 x 2 x 5" pine**
K	2	¼-20 x 3" fh machine screw, nut and washer**
L	2* or 4**	6" dia. plate or stem-type caster
M	3* or 5**	¼-20 x 2½" machine screw, nut, washer
N	1	½" IPT waste nut
O	1	½" IPT x 2¾" nipple
P	1	½" IPT x 90° elbow
Q	1	½" IPT pipe, length to suit
R	1	½" IPT x 45° elbow
S	1	½" IPT x 6" pipe (thread one end only)
T	1	¾" IPT connector
U	1	⅛ x ½ x 2" strap iron
V	2	No. 6-32 x ¼" rh machine screw
W	1	No. 10-32 thumb screw
X	2	¼-20 x 3" fh machine screw, nut, washer

*3-wheel dolly only **4-wheel dolly only

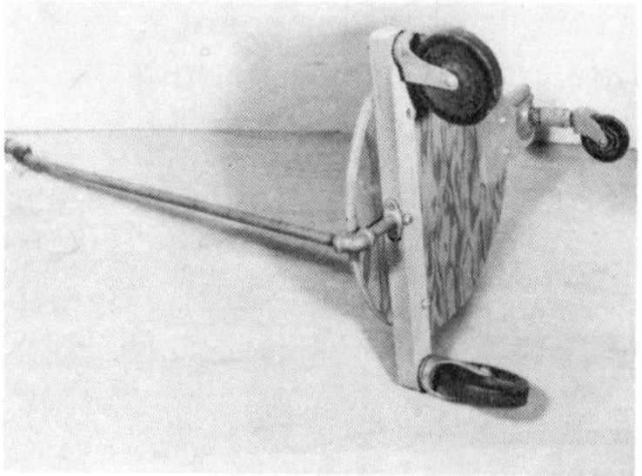

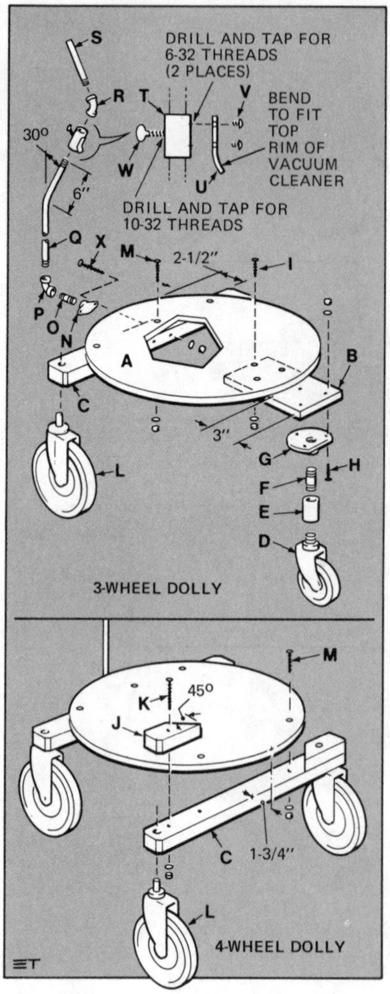
DRILL AND TAP FOR 6-32 THREADS (2 PLACES)
BEND TO FIT TOP RIM OF VACUUM CLEANER
DRILL AND TAP FOR 10-32 THREADS
30°
6"
2-1/2"
3"
3-WHEEL DOLLY
45°
1-3/4"
4-WHEEL DOLLY

Tip-proof vacuum dollies

■ THE TWO VACUUM dollies shown here were designed to roll over typically cluttered shop floors without tipping over. Large-diameter casters and a wide span between wheels do the trick.

Construction is basically the same for both versions. First cut the plywood disc to the diameter of the recess in the bottom of your shop vacuum. If your vacuum has no recess or if you desire extra stability, plan to add the retaining blocks (J) shown on the four-wheel dolly.

Cut the caster-support members and bolt them to the plywood disc. Install the casters and check to be sure the dolly platform is level:

To install the rim-clamp assembly, drill and tap connector (T) as shown and *slide* it onto the upright pipe (Q). Attach strap iron (U), which has been bent to suit the vacuum's top rim. Install the thumbscrew (W) to lock the clamping assembly at the proper height. To remove the vacuum from the dolly, simply loosen the thumbscrew and slide the connector and strap clamp off the rim.

FOLLOW GOOD SAFETY practices with a radial-arm saw: Use goggles to protect eyes from flying particles; wear earmuff-type protectors to reduce saw screech to a safe level; keep sleeves buttoned, and hold work securely. Keep your thumb clearly out of the way as you slowly and steadily pull the saw blade through the work.

Take the hazards out of your home shop

■ HIGH-SPEED cutting edges, kicked-back objects, short circuits and slippery floors do not cause shop accidents—*you* do. Realizing this fact is the biggest step you can take toward making your shop a healthy place in which to work. Once you begin to adopt safe practices and a positive attitude toward safety, old accident-prone habits will begin to die. Your work will probably become more accurate and you will enjoy your time in the shop more.

Living with power tools

According to the U.S. Consumer Product Safety Commission (CPSC), 17,000 persons each year are treated for injuries associated with electrically activated drills, sanders, routers, lathes, grinders, jointers, planers, shapers, welders and soldering guns. Power saws, however, are by far the most likely power tool to be involved in a severe shop accident—approximately 37,000 injuries are reported by hospitals annually. Most are a result of either contact with the blade, electrocution and shock, or projectiles from the material being worked with, usually wood. Investigations prove that most of these mishaps didn't "just happen." Only *you* can take the precautions necessary to prevent them. Learn a few simple rules and techniques and follow them.

1. Study the rule box that is part of this article and post safety reminders wherever you feel they may help. For instance, a sign saying REMOVE CHUCK KEY, posted at your drill press, may keep you from being hit by a ricocheting key if you

SET BLADE depth as shown for safe cutting. The guard is removed for photo clarity only.

A PUSH BLOCK is a must for safety when planing the face of thin stock. It will also improve your work.

CHOOSING the right screwdriver prevents damage to workpiece, blisters and unnecessary strain.

CLAMPING workpieces securely in a vise or to the workbench will make cutting them easier and safer.

WHEN USING sidewall of grinding wheel, protect your eyes and face from flying fragments.

CARRY PORTABLE power tools with fingers off the activating switch to prevent inadvertent start-ups.

PERSONAL SAFEGUARDS

The most expensive tool imaginable is worthless next to you—and yet the most mistreated and abused ''machine'' in many home shops is the human body. The products shown here (and throughout this article) represent a small investment when compared to the money you are apt to pay for health care and insurance. It's foolhardy not to acquire a basic inventory that includes such items as goggles, face shield, a supply of lens cleaner and tissue, muff or plug-type ear protectors, dust mask and respirator with appropriate filter replacements, work gloves and other specialty items necessary for jobs you're likely to do.

COMMON SHOP eye gear is most important (clockwise from top in near photo): face shield, impact goggles, welding cup goggles, chemical splash goggles. Far right, plastic box keeps shop first-aid kit dry and dust-free. One like it should be found in every shop. Included in this one are tweezers, scissors, rubbing alcohol, disinfectant, bandages.

RESPIRATOR and neoprene gloves prevent lung and skin absorption of toxic mists, vapors and compounds.

DUST MASK keeps dust from sanding operations out of your lungs. Wash and/or replace filters as needed.

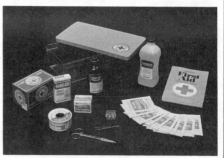

pay attention and notice it after tightening a bit in the drill chuck.

Hand tools are involved in the majority of shop accidents. More than 30,000 people received hospital emergency room treatment for hammer injuries in one year alone. Screwdrivers, manual saws, drills and chisels were not far behind. Aside from hammer-and-thumb type slips caused by miscalculation or loss of concentration, many were the result of misuse and poor technique.

2. Choose the right tool for the job. Improvisation, however ingenious, can lead to danger. Study your hand tools' capabilities and learn their limitations as well. Read relevant literature and make practice runs when performing an unfamiliar operation. Seek personalized instruction when necessary.

3. Well-maintained hand tools shorten job time and are safer to work with. A modest investment in a grinder—or even just in manual jigs for sharpening twist drills and chisels—will keep you from forcing a dull tool to accomplish a task.

4. When things start going wrong, take a break. Don't let yourself be pressured into trying a quick, often disastrous, remedy. Impatience causes accidents. Fatigue is another reason to take a break. When you are tired your reaction time is slower and your eye-hand coordination begins to decline.

5. One of the most severe hand tool accidents occurs when metal is struck against metal and a chip, such as a nailhead, flies into the eye. The importance of protective eyewear cannot be overemphasized.

While a good project design is usually the first concern of serious craftsmen, the design of their shops is often given little thought. Check the following safety criteria.

6. Comfort is critical to safety and efficiency. Keep your shop at a good working temperature. Most people prefer about 60° F. A shop that's too warm tends to make you drowsy and tire more easily. Choose a shop heater with care and follow the maker's instructions when installing. Some gas-fired garage heaters, for example, must be vented to be safe.

7. Adequate lighting also raises your shop's comfort—and safety—index. Use at least two 33-in., 25-watt fluorescent tubes, mounted about 4-ft. above each work station. Baffles and louvers, like the egg-crate designs, reduce glare. As an alternative to fluorescents, use a 150-watt, R-40 flood or spot lamp (with reflector built in) with an adjustable holder. Clamp it so no glare or shadows fall on the work.

Paint walls and ceilings with light, low-gloss washable colors. Keep bulbs and bulb covers clean. Add protective plastic sleeves to fluorescent tubes to contain glass fragments and gas should the tube be broken.

8. Place wall-mounted louvers or an exhaust fan opposite an operable window. A power vent and a supply of fresh air are musts in rooms used for painting and finishing to prevent fire or explosion. Be sure pilot lights, for a gas furnace or hot-water heater, are off when spraying or using flammable materials. Good ventilation (and an appropriate respirator) also prevent inhalation of

---

RULES FOR AVOIDING POWER TOOL ACCIDENTS

■ Be sure electric tools are double-insulated or grounded. A ground fault interrupter is the best protection.

■ "Idiotproof" your shop—if it's accessible to untrained persons and young children—by keeping blades and other sharp accessories out of reach. Install central switch for turning off power to shop circuit and lock it when you leave.

■ Wear appropriate personal protective equipment. Dress comfortably in snug fitting clothing or use a shop apron. Remove jewelry and secure long hair. Do not wear gloves—they can be snagged by cutters, blades and drive belts.

■ Plan your setup carefully: Jigs, clamps, fences and guides, used correctly, make the job easier and safer.

■ Keep all guards, shields and antikickback devices

in place and in operating condition. Replace fatigued springs which no longer snap guards back.

■ Remove chuck keys and wrenches before turning on power. To make this a habit, create a handy place to hang or store them.

■ Be aware of your hands and body. Use a push stick or planing block on narrow or thin work. Never overextend your reach. Stand aside while starting motors—and stand clear of the path of potential kickbacks.

■ Keep power cords out of the way. Keep (and store) extension cords away from oil, heat and sharp objects.

■ Wait until blades or bits are completely stopped before making adjustments. Unplug tool to prevent inadvertent start-ups.

ANTIFATIGUE mats placed at work stations are great leg savers—especially if your shop has a concrete floor.

AUTHOR demonstrates eyewash bottle—a precaution in addition to goggles.

CONTAINER for oily wastes confines highly combustible material until it can be safely removed from the shop.

KEEP BARE bulbs from shattering with clear or low-glare safety globes.

PRESSURE GAUGE on extinguisher (left) indicates when it needs to be recharged. Remote signaling detectors (right) with bedside alarm are ideal for shops that are out of earshot. A smoke detector is a must in any shop.

toxic fumes. Many chemical products are very hazardous—so heed manufacturers' cautions. For example, an ingredient in some paint removers, methylene chloride, forms carbon monoxide in the blood if inhaled.

9. Empty sawdust and combustible waste at the end of every workday. Remember to keep all oily rags in a covered container to prevent spontaneous combustion.

10. Obtain two all-purpose fire extinguishers. Mount one in a central location and the other near an escape route—not next to flammable materials where you might not be able to reach it during a fire.

11. Study your shop floor plan. Does the traffic pattern allow easy, free movement? If not, can it be rearranged? Can unnecessary clutter be removed? A real danger is being startled while you work. Can you rearrange power tools so you face the direction of likely approach? If not, consider locking the door while you work—although this has drawbacks if you work alone.

In any case, act now to take the hazard out of your shop. Don't leave your welfare to chance.

WEAR
SAFETY
GOGGLES

Drilling hard materials

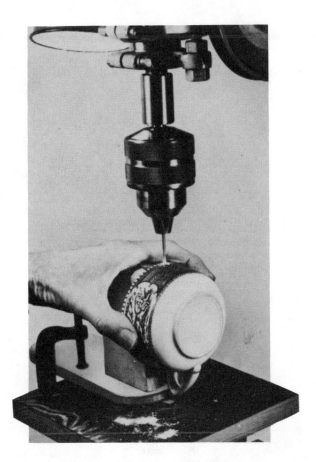

■ A NEW WORLD opens up for many crafts-men when they discover ways of drilling in hard material. Suddenly, a variety of new projects are possible, as more materials become available for the craftsman's use.

Abrasive-grit drilling

An inexpensive method of making a hole in glass, china or similar material is to grind it through with abrasive particles, preferably on a drill press. The bit can be made from rods of aluminum, copper, brass or even a headless nail. As these bits have tubular cutting ends, they are known as "core-type bits." The desired diameter is usually milled in a lathe from a rod, then the bit is center-drilled to form a recess in which cores develop from the material being drilled.

Granular abrasive is used between the material and rotating drill. It is the abrasive that does the actual cutting. Abrasive is usually aluminum-oxide or silicon-carbide grains of 80- to 120-grit size. Types of abrasive include loose grains produced by abrasive manufacturers, value-grinding compound, aluminum-oxide or silicon-carbide grains from "sandpaper." Whatever the abrasive or its source, it is usually mixed with water to make a "soup."

Drill-press speed should be low or moderate for core-type bits. Raise the bit every 10 seconds or so to permit fresh soup to flow over the cutting area. When the hole is almost through, control the feed pressure carefully to prevent chipping on the underside. Don't become discouraged if this method seems exasperatingly slow. Drilling rate depends on such things as hardness of the material being drilled, grit characteristics and drill rpm.

Carbide-alloy drills

A typical masonry drill that's available commercially consists of a steel shank tipped with a flat piece of tungsten carbide. These bits have two cutting edges at a broad angle to each other. So-called "glass drills" are of similar construction, but the carbide pieces are shaped like an arrowhead, the tip angle being smaller (sharper) and the web thinner at the point.

When using carbide-alloy bits, support the glass on a firm surface, such as wood or hardboard, and clamp it securely. Keep the carbide cutter lubricated; a few drops of turpentine serve as a good lubricant. Run the press at moderate speed, and feed the bit carefully to prevent overheating and possible glass breakage. Although the bit can pass easily through the glass, there's a chance that it will cause chipping around the hole as it emerges. To decrease this possibility, turn the glass over as soon as the drill tip emerges (set the depth stop first) and finish drilling from the second side.

Diamond bits

For drilling small, hard gemstones and the like, diamond-studded bits are recommended. A typical set of drills includes 1-, 1¼-, 1½-, 2- and

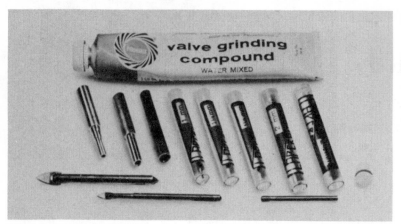

MAKE YOUR OWN BITS like the three at upper left, or buy diamond bits (in plastic tubes) and tungsten-carbide bits (in foreground). Valve-grinding compound holds the abrasive grit when drilling.

BRASS BITS are made on a metal-working lathe. A center hole is being drilled ½ in. deep in a ¼-in.-dia. brass rod. Core bits of this type cut slowly.

A ³⁄₁₆-IN.-DIA. hole is drilled in the bottom half of a glass jar using a brass bit and abrasive compound.

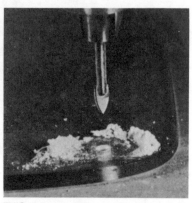

THIS ¼-in. tungsten-carbide bit mounted in a drill press can easily drill through ¼-in. plate glass in minutes.

DRILLING in stones is done with a hobbyist's drill and drill-press stand.

2½-mm sizes. They always should be used wet, with the workpiece being wholly immersed in water or a special drilling fluid.

Sometimes a dam is constructed around the workplace to hold the fluid. This dam is formed with a caulking material or anything else that will make a water-retaining cup.

A small, variable-speed hand grinder is suitable for driving diamond bits in the workshop. When drills are handheld, it is difficult to drill in small, hard objects with precision, but a drill press does make it easy.

To master the technique of using diamond bits, apply pressure carefully to the workpiece until the bit "bites." Then the bit will run without jumping or crawling sideways. Drilling pressure is increased until the drill really starts cutting, as indicated by the appearance of cloudiness in the fluid. Be careful not to apply too much pressure. If the motor slows down, reduce pressure at once: Prolonged pressure can overheat and damage the drill bit. The bit should be backed out frequently—say, every 10 seconds or less—so fluid can refill the hole to cool the tip and clear away loosened solid material.

As in all shop work, take precautions—wear safety glasses while drilling and gloves while handling glass and glass particles.

Drill angled holes accurately

■ DRILLING A HOLE at an angle can be a frustrating job, especially when you're drilling metal. Starting the hole is difficult because the drill bit tends to wander or grab. Finishing the hole is no cinch, either—breaking through can be ticklish, with jamming and bit breakage possible.

But there are tricks that can take some of the headaches out of angle drilling. First, you must provide a surface perpendicular to the drill bit so it can start squarely.

The simplest way to do this is to start drilling with the bit at a right angle to the surface and then tilt either the workpiece or the drill until the desired angle is reached. The latter is done when you're using a portable drill in wood and other soft materials, but locating the hole at a precise point requires care. Another drill-starting trick is to make a center-punch mark at an angle, as shown on the next page.

When using a conical "crater" formed with a drill, start drilling as shown at the left. The width of the crater side (crater radius) should be nearly equal to the diameter of the hole to be drilled.

ANGLE DRILLING is easy when a "crater" is first made with a large twist drill held perpendicular to workpiece (see inset). Punch mark (below) is starter hole for lathe center drill; a twist drill finishes the hole. Wires (below, right) show angles of holes drilled through metal bars and blocks.

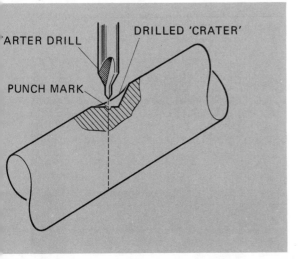

STARTER DRILL   DRILLED 'CRATER'

PUNCH MARK

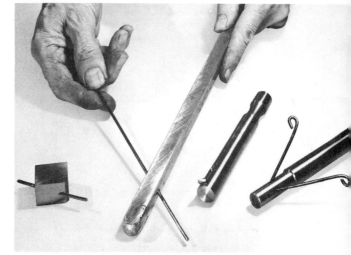

After making a punch mark at the desired location, begin drilling with a regular lathe center drill. Select a "stubby" one since a steeply angled surface may cause a twist drill to grab at the corners.

With the drilled-crater technique, it may be desirable to use initially a twist drill that is slightly smaller than the finished diameter of the hole. Best results with this method will be obtained when the hole is perpendicular or nearly perpendicular to the crater side.

The use of a machined groove for a starting land, shown below, right, is especially helpful when several holes are to be drilled at the same distance from the end of a rod and at the same angle to its axis. The groove can subsequently be removed by machining the bar to a smaller size, as was done with the one before.

Although it is not practical to make too deep a hole with an end mill, it can be used to make a very neat starting recess.

If a number of identical workpieces are to be drilled, a jig can be made to speed the job of starting and drilling holes at the same angle.

The methods shown on these pages should produce accurate results if care is taken in locating the starting surface and in positioning the punch mark. Once started, drilling should go smoothly until the bit breaks through. The be-

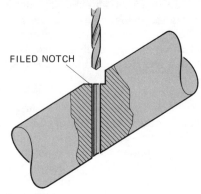

FILED NOTCH

WHEN NOTCH IS FILED or sawed in bar with one side perpendicular to hole axis, it provides flat surface for drill. The technique works fine when finished look is unimportant. Punch mark and the use of lathe center drill give the most accurate start.

ANGLED PUNCH MARK helps start a drill when angle and hole size are both small. To keep the bit from drifting, the entire drill tip should contact the punch mark.

MACHINED GROOVE is a variation of the notch method. Starting surface can be turned at any angle, but groove must be wide enough for drill clearance.

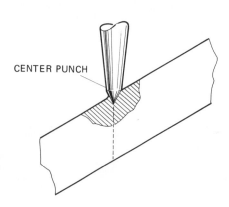

CENTER PUNCH

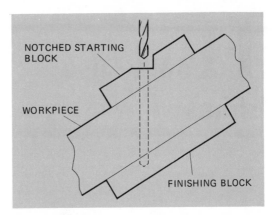

STARTING BLOCK of scrap material, notched to angle desired, is clamped to workpiece; a finishing block clamped underneath assures clean drill breakthrough.

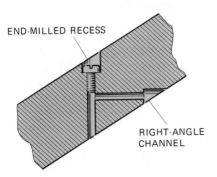

END-MILLING A RECESS is the neatest way to provide a starting surface for drill. When hole is to accommodate a pan-head screw, recess is milled slightly larger than diameter of head, which seats squarely against flat. Right-angled channel is typical use of method.

BORING BAR for lathe is made using the end-mill technique. Grind cutting bit from high-speed steel, tap hole to receive 1/4-20 Allen setscrew for locking bit.

ginning of this moment can usually be felt and often heard. Feed slowly and carefully at this point, until the drill emerges completely and runs free. If bit jamming is a recurrent problem, clamp a piece of scrap material to the bottom of the workpiece for the drill to continue into, so that it will leave a clean-edged hole on the workpiece.

A scrap block can also be used to aid starting (top, right). When no finishing block is used, there are usually some irregular fragments (burrs) to trim away from the bottom of the hole.

Secure clamping of the workpiece is important in angled drilling, since bit pressure will tend to swing the workpiece downward. When using a progression of drills of several different sizes, start each drill carefully to prevent grabbing. Generous use of cutting oil is also helpful. And wearing a face shield or goggles for protection from flying chips is not just a good idea—it's a must.

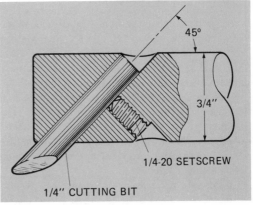

How to use shims

DRIVE THE SHIMS across each other. This will effectively raise the board as much as you want.

■ NOT MANY building materials come perfectly straight or perfectly even. Not many houses are perfectly level or plumb. This situation is referred to as "conditions in the field."

The total effect is that when you install a window, the sill may be out of level, or when you hang a door, the jamb may not be plumb. You may also run into the same trouble when you frame a new addition. To solve these and other field condition problems, use shims.

A shim is a small piece of material, usually wood, that will make up a small discrepancy in measurements. They are usually made out of the

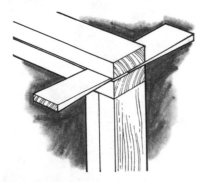

SHIM FROM BOTH sides of the work. This will help to keep the board level and stable.

same material that they are supporting. Where great compression can be expected (like a girder resting on a masonry footing) a static material like slate is used. The most common shimming material is wooden shingle points.

The most common mistake in shimming is to drive a single shingle point in from one side. This frequently results in an uneven and unstable condition. The beauty of shingle shims is that use of a pair together produces automatic leveling. Here's how it's done:

First, split up a shingle to make 2 or 3-inch-wide pieces. Then start the thin edges toward

each other from opposite sides of the board. Drive them in so they meet in the center under the board. Here, you might find that backing one up with a block and sharply tapping the other will help the thin points overlap. Now you can put your level on the board and check the bubble as you tap the shingles—first one, then the other. With gentle taps you can raise a board in very fine degrees until you get exactly the right amount of rise to a level condition. Don't worry about the excess shingle—it's easily trimmed. Firmly score the edge of the shingle flush to the board with a razor knife. A sharp blow from the opposite side will break it off cleanly. If most of the shingle has been driven through, and only a

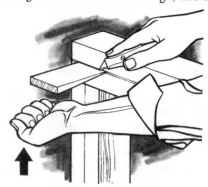

TRIM OFF excess by first scoring with knife. This will keep edge flush for sheetrock or siding.

few inches of the thickest part remain, you should trim it with a handsaw.

It's really a simple process worth doing carefully. Remember, you don't need shims to rectify a mistake, although they are great for that purpose if you really build yourself into a problem. Careful shimming on the frame will save you a lot of time and a lot of headaches when you start to put up sheetrock and trim.

JIG MAKES fast work of many angles including standard 45° miters and 15° and 30° cuts.

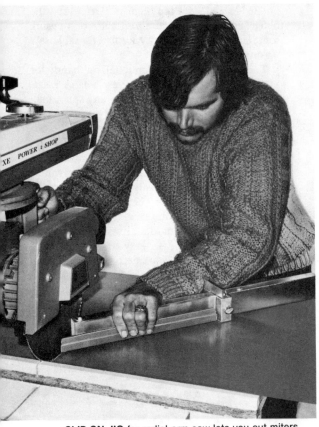

SLIP-ON JIG for radial-arm saw lets you cut miters while leaving the blade set at 90°.

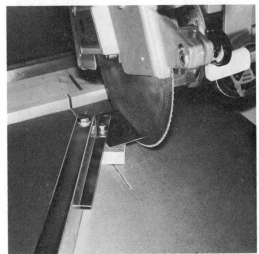

FENCE POSITIONS are gauged with arm protractors positioned tightly against flat of the blade.

Miter boards

RADIAL SAW MITER BOARD

Here's an auxiliary table with an adjustable fence that lets you cut 15°, 30°, 45°, and 90° angles with the radial-arm saw in the 90° position. Other angle positions can be added to the jig if desired. Cutting may be done from either side of the jig's adjustable fence (E). This enables you to choose the straight, nonrounded side of the work for holding against the fence while making the cut.

Construct the jig as shown in the plans. You may want to add a stop block to the board underside. Locate the block so the miter board will reposition in exactly the same place each time it is used.

The holes bored through the adjustable fence should be made using a drill press or a portable drill in a portable-drill guide. Bore one (pivot hole) near the end of the fence. Bore second hole at a point which falls above miter-board surface in all positions, 0 to 45°.

Next, mark the pivot hole in miter board and align with pivot hole in fence. Using the latter to guide hand-held drill, bore hole in board. Install Teenut at bottom of pivot hole and fasten the miter fence to the board with a bolt.

Clamp fence in each angle position and use the near hole in fence to guide drill through miter board. Counterbore for Teenuts in the board's

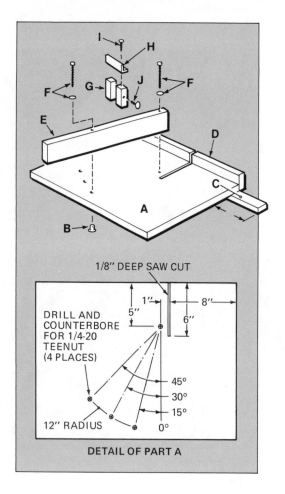

1/8" DEEP SAW CUT

DRILL AND
COUNTERBORE
FOR 1/4-20
TEENUT
(4 PLACES)

1"
5"
8"
6"

45°
30°
15°
0°

12" RADIUS

DETAIL OF PART A

WEAR
SAFETY
GOGGLES

underside and then tap them in. Determine the fence angles, using an arm protractor or by using some simple trigonometry. (See text for table-saw jig on next page.)

The guide-fence stop is optional, but handy for production cuts. The thumbscrew acts as a set-screw and will secure the stop in any spot along the fence.

The same jig design can be adapted to your bandsaw. With the bandsaw miter board, however, the board moves with the work into the saw blade. A slide must be fastened to the miter-board underside, so it will ride snugly in the saws's miter groove. The most convenient operating position, in this case, is to stand behind the blade and pull board and workpiece toward you. In this manner, it's easy to see where the blade will enter the workpiece. A drawer pull fastened to the board for righthand use makes the action easy and balanced.

MATERIALS LIST—RADIAL-SAW JIG		
Key	No.	Size and description (use)
A	1	¾ × 18 × 24" countertop scrap or plywood (table)
B	4	¼-20 Teenut
C	1	⅜ × ¾ × 29" or to suit
D	1	¾ × 2¼ × 24" pine (fixed fence)
E	1	5/4 × 2 × 18" hardwood or bend from sheet metal (adjustable fence)
F	2	¼-20 × 2¾" hex hd. bolts, washers
G	2	1 × 1 × 2" hardwood, aluminum or steel (stops)
H	1	⅛ × 1 × 1 × 3⅛" angle iron or aluminum
I	2	¾" No. 8 machine screw (or rh wood screw if stops are made of wood)
J	1	¼-20 × 1½" thumbscrew

JIG TABLE was made from sink cutout, available at most cabinet dealers.

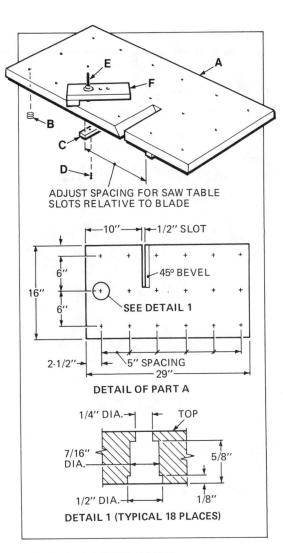

ADJUST SPACING FOR SAW TABLE
SLOTS RELATIVE TO BLADE

10" — 1/2" SLOT

45° BEVEL

6"

16"

SEE DETAIL 1

6"

2-1/2" — 5" SPACING
29"

DETAIL OF PART A

1/4" DIA. — TOP

7/16" DIA.

5/8"

1/2" DIA. 1/8"

DETAIL 1 (TYPICAL 18 PLACES)

TABLE SAW MITER BOARD

Conventional miter gauges are usually too small to allow a secure grip on large workpieces. Solid clamps, plus the large surface area of this sliding miter board, make cutting precise angles a sure thing.

Compound angle cutting is also possible, since the jig's blade slot is beveled 45° on the side toward which your blade tilts.

When building the jig, take care to make the slides, which fit miter-gauge grooves, absolutely perpendicular to the board's front edge. The workpiece-holding clamps are built onto the board and can be repositioned as the task demands.

Angle-cutting positions must be measured with an arm protractor. Commonly used angles can be marked on masking tape or permanently scribed on the surface of the board.

A good way to determine accurate fence posi-

WITH GUIDES mounted in 45° positions, miters can be cut at both ends of molding without readjustment.

USE CLAMP to hold the work rigid. This is especially important when making compound miter cuts.

tions is to use simple trigonometry. The tangent function will give you the ratio to locate appropriate sets of coordinates for any angle 0 to 90°. To do so, look up the tangent function for the angle in question. The tangent of 60°, for example, is 1.732. This means that for every inch you measure from the vertex along the line adjacent to the angle (blade's path), you should measure 1.732 in. to the right or left on a line perpendicular to the blade's path. If you measure 8 in. from the vertex on the blade's path, you should measure 1.732 in. x 8, or 13⅞-in. to the right or left from the 8-in. mark. Connect this point to the vertex, using a straight line to find the fence position for 60°.

MATERIALS LIST—TABLE-SAW JIG		
Key	No.	Size and description (use)
A	1	¾ × 16 × 29" plywood or countertop scrap (table)
B	18	¼-20 thread inserts
C	2	¼ × ¾ × 16" pine
D	6	¾" No. 8 fh screw
E	as reqd.	¼-20 threaded rod, washer, nut
F	as reqd.	¾" stock (clamps)

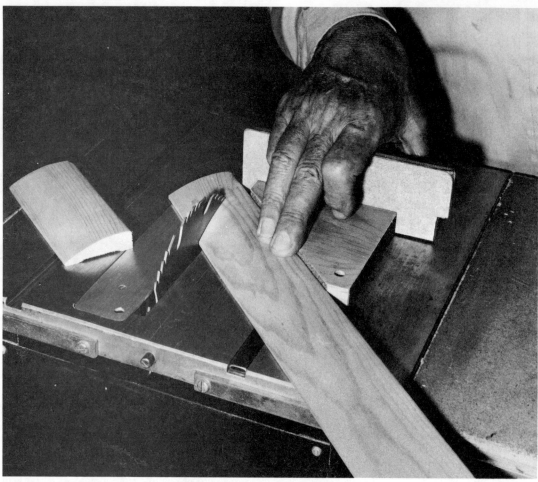

ANGLE BLOCKS save time, assure accuracy. Blade guard is removed for photos. Do not operate your saw without the blade guard.

Angle blocks for miter cuts

■ MITERED JOINTS demand accuracy. Even a slight miscalculation will inevitably compound itself into a conspicuous, wedge-shaped gap in your finished work. Not only is this frustrating and shoddy-looking, but it's also expensive if you choose to try again and redo it.

A set of blocks for common angle cutting will take only half an hour to make from scrap plywood. They'll help you minimize waste and save hours of job time. No longer will you have to adjust and readjust your miter gauge every time you change from making a right-hand to a left-hand cut. Set it at 90° and move the miter gauge and block from one side to the other—or remove the block to cut at 90°.

The photos show how to hold and use the blocks. *Note: The blade guard has been removed for photo clarity only.* Be sure the block does not contact the blade—the garnet paper will dull it.

To make the blocks, cut a 6x8-in. rectangle and a 6x6-in. square from ¾-in. plywood. Make certain one corner of each is a true right angle. The easiest place to get a perfect 90° corner is from the mill-cut corner of a plywood sheet. Lacking that, set your gauge with a dependable square and cut your own. Also check your blade with the square to be certain you are making a true vertical cut.

Reset gauge

Next, reset your miter gauge to the block angle you intend to cut first (45° or 30°). Use the appropriate draftsman's triangle with its long side butted against the fully exposed width of your blade (see photo). On a set-tooth blade, where teeth alternately point in opposite directions, be certain that contact is made at equivalent points on two teeth pointing in the *same* direction. The miter gauge is then set flush to the opposite side of the triangle as shown above.

Proceed to make your cuts. Trim ¾ in. off all acute angle corners to provide additional clearance between block and blade while cutting. Use contact cement to adhere ⅝-in.-wide strips of 80-grit garnet paper to edges. Finally, drill a hole in one corner of each block for hanging near your saw where they can be easily reached whenever you need them.

Adapt for radial-arm saw

These blocks can also be adapted for use on a radial-arm saw. Simply place a board between the fence and the block to provide clearance for the cut-off end. The advantage is that you won't have to lift and swing the blade out of the 90° groove, then lower it into the angled groove each time the direction of cut is changed.

GARNET PAPER edging helps keep block and workpiece from slipping or "creeping" as you cut.

FOR TRUE angles on the blocks, use draftsman's triangles to set the miter gauge for cutting.

SAFELY POSITION fingers when mitering narrow picture-frame moldings as shown here.

THE 45° ANGLE block makes mitering door or window casings quick, easy and accurate.

Shop tips

Jigsaw sanding

You may be aware of the jigsaw's versatility as a cutting tool, but with this easy-to-make attachment, it can perform sanding operations as well.

Insert the wood-screw threads of a ¼-in.-dia. x 2-in. hanger bolt into the end of a ¾ x 1½ x 3-in. wood block. Then use rubber cement to glue abrasive paper to both faces of the block. Glue coarse grit on one side, medium on the other. Or use adhesive-backed paper.

For sanding, place the protruding machine-screw threads in the saw's lower chuck. Use different-shaped blocks for specific sanding operations.

Dimple-free nailing

Prevent accidental hammer dimples on wood surfaces with this handy protective shield. Cut the shield from ⅟₁₆-in.-thick plastic laminate and bore a ⅛-in.-dia. centered hole as shown.

To use, start the nail, then place the shield over the nail. Hold the shield flat against the workpiece face and drive the nail until it's flush with the laminate.

Remove the shield and use a nailset to drive the projecting nailhead flush with or below the workpiece surface, as desired.

MOUNT THE SANDING BLOCK in the saw's lower chuck. Remove blade guide for easy access.

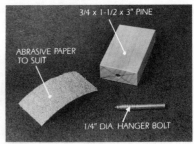

THE SANDING BLOCK is ready for assembly. Note the block's centerbored pilot hole.

Truing board edges

To successfully edge-glue two boards, their mating edges must be perfectly true. Dressed lumber is rarely purchased with edges suitable for joining. Here is a quick and foolproof method you can use to true the edges of any two boards—simultaneously.

Clamp the boards with their mating edges butted together tightly. Then, using a straightedge guide and a portable circular saw, cut straight through the center of the joint, removing stock from both boards.

If the gap between the boards is wider than the saw kerf, repeat the procedures as many times as necessary to close the gap. The result will be two straight and true mating edges that will produce an "invisible" joint.

STEER THE SAW along a straightedge guide. Arrows indicate unevenness in board edges.

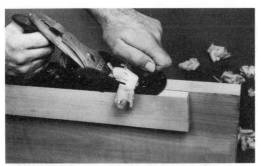

DURING PLANNING, keep the guide flat against the workpiece's face.

1-1/4" NO. 8 SHEET METAL SCREW (2 REQD.)

3/4" STOCK, WIDTH AND LENGTH TO SUIT

HOLE DRILLED TO SUIT SCREW (2 REQD.)

HERE'S THE GUIDE prior to mounting. Note the iron-clearing notch.

Plane guide

This simple bench plane guide can aid you in planing perfectly square edges. Choose a square-edge piece of ¾-in. stock for the guide and cut it 3 in. longer than the plane. The guide's width often is determined by the job, but a 2½-in. width will be sufficient for most work. Cut a ⅛-in.-deep x ½-in. notch in the guide's top edge. The notch will allow the guide to clear the protruding plane iron (blade) and sit flat against the plane's bottom. Next, bore two ³⁄₁₆-in.-dia. mounting holes through the plane's base. Attach the guide to the plane with two 1¼-in. No. 8 sheet-metal screws.

To use, simply keep the guide flat against the workpiece's face while planing. The plane will cut perpendicular to the guide, forming a square edge.

Radial sawdust slot

Sawdust that collects along a radial-arm saw fence can cause inaccurate cutting. The sawdust forms small mounds, preventing the workpiece from abutting the fence tightly. To eliminate this problem, provide a sawdust escape slot between the fence and the worktable.

Make the sawdust slot by nailing ⅛ x ¾ x 1-in. softwood spacer blocks along the fence. Place the blocks 6 in. apart, but don't put one directly under the saw-blade path. Position the fence on the saw with the spacer blocks facing forward. Tighten the fence lock knobs and be sure the spacer blocks are below the worktable's surface.

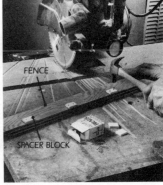

FENCE

SPACER BLOCK

Hinging a plywood edge

Boring straight pilot holes into the edge of fir plywood for a continuous hinge can be tricky. The drill bit often is deflected off course when it hits a glued joint, a dense knot or a void in the plywood's edge.

To solve this problem, nail a ⅛-in.-thick pine reinforcement strip to the plywood's edge. Then tape the hinge in place over the pine strip. Punch screw-hole center marks and bore pilot holes through the strip and into the plywood edge. The pine strip will serve to support the drill bit and keep it straight. Remove the strip before installing the hinge.

This technique is also useful for installing other styles of hinges and hardware on delicate surfaces.

CUT RINGS by using two saw blades at once.

Cutting rings

Cutting solid rings using a sabre saw or jigsaw is time-consuming. But with a multiple-blade hole saw and a drill, you can cut perfectly round rings quickly and easily.

Mount two blades in the hole saw's toolhead at the same time. Select two saw blades that will produce a ring of the desired thickness and diameter. This technique works with both a portable electric drill and a drill press.

PLACE DOWEL in drill and contour with file.

Turning small diameters

Here's a way to turn small-diameter, decorative finials and spindles on a drill press.

First, select the desired diameter wood dowel and chuck it in the drill press. Then, using a variety of files, rasps and abrasive tapes and cords, contour the dowel to the desired shape. Use very fine-grit abrasive paper for the finishing touches.

For best results, run the drill at its highest speed.

Double-duty disc

Unless you happen to have two disc sanders in your shop (an expensive luxury), switching from rough to smooth sanding requires changing the discs. But this trick provides you with two differ-

ent sanding surfaces on one disc sander.

Using a circular template and a razor knife, simultaneously cut out the centers of two sanding discs—one coarse grit, one medium.

Glue the outer ring from one disc and the center portion of the other to the disc sander. Now you can sand both rough and smooth finishes on the same machine. Use the cutoff pieces in reverse order when it's time to replace the sanding surface.

GLUE SECTIONS from two different abrasive grits for both smooth and rough sanding.

Splinterless dadoes

Cutting dadoes will often tear and splinter the crossgrain on a piece of wood. This is especially true of plywood veneer.

To prevent this, score two lines just outside the lines-of-cut with a sharp razor knife. The scored lines will allow the wood's grain to "break off" cleanly as the cutting tool passes. The result is splinterless dadoes and a more professional-looking joint.

This technique is effective with all varieties of dado-cutting tools, including routers, shapers and either radial-arm or table saws with dado heads.

Change splintered dadoes (left) to smooth dadoes.

Low-cost shelves

Here's a simple way to add shelving to your workshop, garage, office or pantry. The shelves are designed for low cost and ease of fit. But they also have some real advantages over conventional support systems.

The suspending flange strengthens the entire length of the shelf, in the same way an angle section is stronger than a flat. The suspending flange also protects the wall from damage when awkward loads are shelved. And heavy loading actually increases the shelf contact with the wall, instead of causing the shelf to sag away from the wall, as with most other supporting methods.

It's important to use only plywood for the wall flange. Inexpensive off-cut strips can be bought at a lumberyard. The shelf must be both glued and nailed (or screwed) to the wall flange. Use wood glue and generous-size common nails, after boring pilot holes.

The table gives suggested widths and thicknesses for the shelves and wall flanges. You can vary dimensions to suit the scrap material you have.

As with all shelving, be sure the wall fastener is secure. For larger shelves fixed to wall studs, use two screws per stud, one above the other. For brick or concrete block walls, space the screws along the top edge of the wall flange at about 12-in. intervals. Finally, be careful not to overload the shelves.

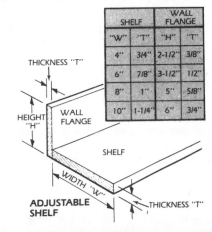

SHELF		WALL FLANGE	
"W"	"T"	"H"	"T"
4"	3/4"	2-1/2"	3/8"
6"	7/8"	3-1/2"	1/2"
8"	1"	5"	5/8"
10"	1-1/4"	6"	3/4"

Miterbox guides

Two sections of angle iron fastened to the top of a miterbox can keep the saw at the appropriate angle to the workpiece. Fasten angle iron sections at the 45° slot spaced apart slightly more than the width of the saw band. You can also use a pair of guides at the 90° slot.

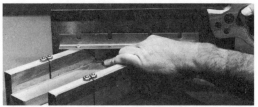

Miterbox holder

A section of heavy angle iron fastened to the bottom of a miterbox can make the box much easier to use. The angle iron, cut to the length of the miterbox, should be clamped in a shop vise. The box will remain stationary, leaving both hands free to manipulate the work and to make the cut.

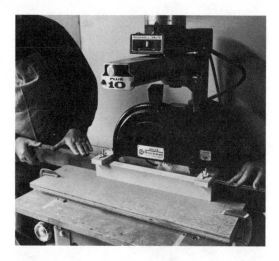

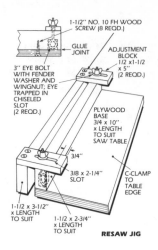

1-1/2" NO. 10 FH WOOD SCREW (8 REQD.)

GLUE JOINT

ADJUSTMENT BLOCK 1/2 x1-1/2 x 5" (2 REQD.)

3" EYE BOLT WITH FENDER WASHER AND WINGNUT; EYE TRAPPED IN CHISELED SLOT (2 REQD.)

PLYWOOD BASE 3/4 x 10" x LENGTH TO SUIT SAW TABLE

3/4"

3/8 x 2-1/4" SLOT

C-CLAMP TO TABLE EDGE

1-1/2 x 3-1/2" x LENGTH TO SUIT

1-1/2 x 2-3/4" x LENGTH TO SUIT

RESAW JIG

Resaw jig

This jig was developed to resaw the stock in order to double the covering capacity of a ¾ x 3 in.-wide cedar paneling. The jig was designed for a radial-arm saw but works equally well on table and band saws.

The throat pieces are of 1½-in.-thick material. There is no depth limit within reason for band saws, but for radial-arm and table saws, limit depth to the blade capacity minus ¼ in. Cut the back throat pieces from a 2 x 4. The front throat is a 2 x 4 ripped to 2¾ in. wide. It has two slots bored and chiseled to receive eyebolts.

Make the jig as long as your saw table can accommodate. Size the plywood piece so its's flush with the table edge. The plywood serves as a way to fasten the jig securely to the saw table with C-clamps.

Cut two adjustment blocks. Use a drill and sabre saw to make slots for the threaded ends of the eyebolts. Position the eyebolts in their slots and assemble the front throat pieces to the plywood base with glue and four 1½-in., No. 10 flathead wood screws. Attach the back throat to one end of the adjustment blocks with glue and screws. Run the threaded end of the eyebolts through the slots in the adjustment blocks, then add washers and wingnuts.

To use the jig, first adjust the throat so the stock slides through snugly but freely. Center the space between the throat pieces on the saw blade and secure the jig with C-clamps. Test the cut for accuracy and readjust if needed. Feed stock at a uniformly slow rate so you achieve an attractive resaw pattern and avoid jamming the saw.

Saw platform

Use your miterbox as a platform to support small pieces of wood while you're cutting them with a sabre saw. The sabre saw blade won't strike the bottom of the miterbox, and the sides are close enough to support even very thin wood pieces while you're cutting them.

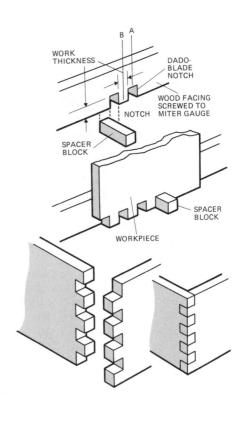

Spacing jig

With a spacing jig attached to the miter gauge, it's a simple trick to cut a perfect-fitting box or finger joint on your own table saw. The jig is little more than a wood fence screw-fastened to the gauge and fitted with a small projecting block which uniformly spaces a series of notches across the width of the work. The notches are made with a dado cutter, and their width and depth are generally equal to or slightly less than the thickness of the stock. With ½-in.-thick stock, the notches will be ½ in. wide, ½ in. deep and ½ in. apart.

To make the joint, stand the two pieces to be joined against the fence so the edge of one piece is even with line A and the edge of the other is even with B. Push the work across the cutter, then shift it so the notch just cut sits over the spacing block, and make a second notch. Place the second notch over the block and make a third notch and so on. Repeat the step until notches are made the full width of the work.

It is important that the two pieces of stock are held in the same position throughout the notching. This is assured when the spacer block pro-

jects far enough to catch both pieces. If desired, the two pieces can be clamped together with a small C-clamp. Adjustments can be made by moving either the spacer block or the fence itself to give you the perfect fit on your joint.

Dishes from a table saw

If you want to dish a disc, but don't have a lathe, there's another way to form a saucer-like cavity—with your table saw. All you need is a V-notched board clamped to the saw and positioned so it centers the blank directly over the vertical axis of the blade. With blade running below the table and the disc face down in the V-notch, crank up the blade ⅛ in. into the work and slowly rotate the disc 360°. You should begin to feel the blade cutting into the wood. Raise the blade another ⅛ in. and repeat the procedure.

By taking a number of light cuts and slowly rotating the work each time, you'll produce a perfectly concave dish requiring very little sanding. If you want a cut which has a smaller diameter, try using a smaller blade. Remember, the sharper the blade, the better cut you will get.

Wedge-cutting jig

If you must cut a lot of wedges, you can mass-cut them in jig time by using a notched board. The board is notched as shown to suit the desired taper, and the saw fence is set so the blade just clears the jig as it's passed along the fence. Sawing is done with the grain after the stock is first crosscut from wide material.

As each wedge is cut, the stock is flopped in the notch. Like slicing cheese, the jig is pushed forward, then withdrawn with the wedge in the notch. Select stock free of knots and with straight grain. If you use a hollow-ground combination blade, there will be no need to sand the wedges. Width of the stock from which the wedges are cut must equal the length of the notch so the wedges will have chisel points. If blunt points are wanted, make the notch in the board deeper.

Boring long holes

How do you bore a hole completely through a board edgewise that's 2 in. or so wider than the bit is long? You bore from opposite edges. In doing so, there's a trick to keeping the two holes aligned and here's how:

Clamp a scrap board to the drill-press table and bore a hole in it ½-in. deep. Then lower the table and bore a hole 3 in. deep in the edge of the work. Replace the bit with a long dowel of the same size. Align the dowel with the hole in the wood table by lowering the chuck, then lock the table. Put the original bit back in the chuck, insert a short dowel pin in the hole in the wood table, place the work over the pin and bore down from the top edge to meet the first hole. If you have carefully followed the correct procedure, both holes will be on target and align perfectly.

 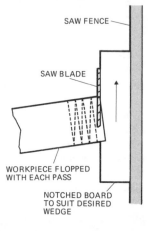

SAW FENCE

SAW BLADE

WORKPIECE FLOPPED
WITH EACH PASS

NOTCHED BOARD
TO SUIT DESIRED
WEDGE

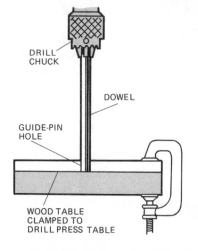

DRILL
CHUCK

DOWEL

GUIDE-PIN
HOLE

WOOD TABLE
CLAMPED TO
DRILL PRESS TABLE

Homemade tenoner

You can buy a tenoner that slides in the groove of your saw table and has a special clamping fixture to hold the work, or you can make one that rides the fence and uses a common C-clamp as shown here. Both are used to make the cheek cuts on a tenon after the shoulder cuts have already been completed.

When a single blade is used, the work can simply be turned edge for edge to make a second cheek cut. If you use two blades with a spacer between, one pass is all that is necessary and you're done. If your saw's fence is a simple box channel like the one shown in the photo on the right, the tenoner is made to fit it like a saddle with scant clearance to ride without binding and without play. Waxing the inside will help it slide easier. In following the dimensions, note that the tunnel is dimensioned for a 1-in.-thick fence and will vary in size with the particular fence you have. Note too that the vertical stop against which the work is placed, then clamped, must be at a right angle to the base to give you a properly cut tenon to fit your project.

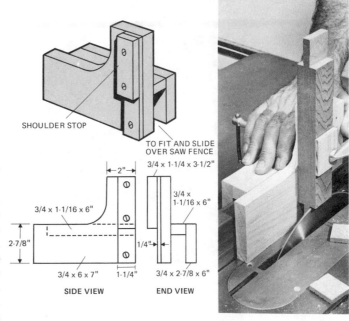

SHOULDER STOP

TO FIT AND SLIDE OVER SAW FENCE

3/4 x 1-1/4 x 3-1/2"

3/4 x 1-1/16 x 6"

3/4 x 1-1/16 x 6"

2"

2-7/8"

1/4"

3/4 x 6 x 7" 1-1/4"

3/4 x 2-7/8 x 6"

SIDE VIEW END VIEW

Setting blade height

While you can set blade height by the saw's built-in scale, it's often quicker to do it with a stepped gauge block comprising a number of 1/8-in. thick plywood strips glued together in a stack. Each strip is 1/2 or 3/4-in. shorter than the next. To use the block, you place it over the blade and crank the blade down (or up) until the block rests flat on the table. For example, if you want to set the blade 3/4 in. high, you pick the sixth step.

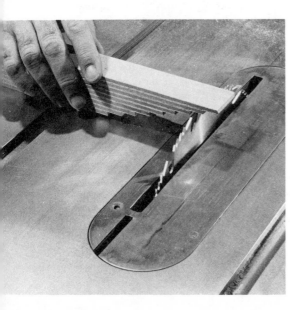

Spiral-kerf dowels

The best-holding glue dowels are dowels which have a spiral kerf. Not only does the kerf help line the hole with glue from top to bottom, but it affords an escape for glue trapped in the bottom of the hole when clamps are applied. To kerf a glue dowel on a bandsaw, tilt table 15°, clamp the miter gauge to it and slowly rotate the dowel as the blade cuts a 1/16-in.-deep kerf. Don't attempt this with a short length of dowel.

Double-duty bandsaw

While a bandsaw is primarily for cutting irregular shapes, it still has other potential. Here it is being used for quantity cutoff work even though it has no fence or a groove for a miter gauge. As shown in the setup above, a scrap of wood is clamped to the table to serve as a fence and a wood block pinch-hits for a miter gauge. In use, narrow stock is guided squarely through the blade by the backup block used as a pusher. To maintain a high level of accuracy it is suggested that you make the block as perfectly square as is possible.

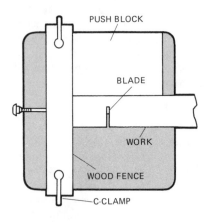

Spring board for table saw ripping

When work must be held in close contact with the fence for the entire length of a cut, the spring action of a spring board can often prove to be much better than the hand. It's simply made by sawing a 60° angle at the end of a hardwood scrap. Then rip several closely spaced "fingers" one-third its length. To use it, clamp it to the saw table. As you feed the wood through the saw the fingers will hold the piece to be cut in contact with the fence by bearing lightly against the wood.

Beginners do it. Journeyman carpenters do it. Even mastercraftsmen do it. No one who tackles home repairs or has a workshop is immune to an occasional workworking snafu. The professional falls back upon his experience—time-proven steps and methods that will get him out of trouble with comparative ease. You can, too.

On these pages, we have collected some of the most common workshop problems, and the solutions for extricating yourself from them. The answers come from a number of professionals who were happy to share the techniques they use to get their jobs back on the track again.

Embedded screw

With a ⅛-in. bit, bore holes straight down all around the screw shaft. In softwood, puncture with a thin finishing nail. A little digging may be needed to get needlenose or locking pliers around the top of the shaft. Twist and pull.

If you can't mar the wood, drill a hole in the center of the shank, about one-third the shank's diameter. Pick a screw extractor to fit the hole; set extractor head in a socket or tap wrench; insert head and turn wrench counterclockwise. Reverse threads on the extractor bite into the inside of the screw shaft, forcing it to turn. This also works on a shorn bolt in an engine head.

IF SURFACE damage is no problem, bore holes around shank of screw.

GRAB SCREW with square or needle-nose pliers and twist counterclockwise.

TO AVOID damaging surface around screw, drill hole in shank. Start at angle if surface is uneven.

INTO screw-shank hole, insert screw extractor set in tap wrench. Twist counterclockwise. Sets are about $1 from Brookstone Co., Vose Farm Rd., Peterborough, NH 03458.

Broken drill bit

The first thing to do is to file away the burrs on the protruding tip of whatever is left of the broken bit. Then, you can rechuck this piece and continue the drilling procedure, if possible.

If this doesn't work, there's another solution to the problem. File a spade tip on a nail of the same diameter as the broken bit. Then, cut off the nailhead, insert the revised bit (the nail) in your drill chuck, tighten securely and resume the drilling.

Stuck drawers

Locate a retail outlet that sells desiccants (chemical dying agents) such as silica gel or calcium chloride. Well-stocked hardware stores often carry them.

Now, buy a plastic trash bag large enough to enclose the chest, or make your own sealed cover with a polyethylene dropcloth and tape. Put the pack of humidity-absorbing chemical in a saucer on the chest. Cover everything with the plastic and seal tightly with tape. Wait about 48 hours. Unseal the bag. The chemicals should have absorbed enough moisture—the culprit that makes drawers stick—to loosen them.

If this doesn't work, examine each one of the drawers. Use a piece of 220-grit abrasive to sand scuffed areas where drawers bind. Sand scuffed areas in the cabinet also.

Miscut mortise

If you have plenty of frame stock, simply cut another length. If not, carefully measure the width and angle of the joint undercut area. From any leftover scraps, cut a slightly oversize section to fit the gap.

Once the drawers slide out as they did in the drier weather, put a coat of clear, glossy polyurethane varnish over the drawer interiors.

This may sound easy, but it isn't. Cutting that tight an angle takes a lot more skill than most people have. It would probably be easier to use plumber's epoxy and mold the stuff into the joint. This is meant for wood frames that you plan to paint.

POSITION members with square. Measure gap. From same framing stock, cut piece slightly oversize to fill gap.

End splits

Force a thin line of carpenter's glue in the crack; remove the nail. Wood tends to return to its original form, so it will press sides of the crack together. When glue sets, bore a hole slightly less than the diameter of the nail and renail through this hole.

Predrill holes for all fastening near the edge of a wood member.

Lost nailhead

There are several solutions. You can set the shank below the surface with a nailset and fill the hole with wood putty. If the nail must be removed, start driving the shaft down with a nailset, then force it through the other side of the wood member with a nail of the same diameter, the tip of which you've clipped off with a hack-saw. Then pull out the shank from the other side.

If the shank juts above the surface, grip it with locking pliers and rock the pliers back on the outer curve of the jaws. This produces the same action as a hammer's claw.

If you run into this problem often, you might want to get a tool that's specifically designed to yank out headless nails.

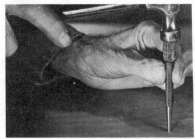

STRAIGHTEN protruding shank and set it well below surface with nailset. Fill hole and sand smooth.

IF NAIL must be removed, cut tip off nail of same size or file tip flat. Use nail to drive embedded nail through far enough on other side to pull it out.

Limited space for wrench

This is a tough one. If the job doesn't require that the nut be tightened to the maximum, chances are you can reach in and push the nut finger-tight. But, if it must be absolutely secure, you can try holding it with an adjustable-grip or needle-nose pliers while you turn the machine screw or bolt with the appropriate tool. To keep the plier jaws from slipping off the nut, wrap a turn or two of masking or friction tape over the serrated jaw surfaces.

For those jobs where this stunt won't work, you should consider adding a specialty tool to your toolbox. The tool is only 1%6 in. high. With it, you can tighten a nut with your hand on the wheel at all times; the ratchet allows you to turn the handle without removing your hand from the tool.

CUTAWAY shows tight spot that is ideal for ratchet drive.

Splintered cuts

Using a backup board is the usual way to minimize splintered edges. But for this to work, the boards must be clamped together tightly. Since clamps are often unavailable at the job site, you can make do with masking tape. Press the tape securely to the plywood on the back side of the cut. The cut won't be absolutely clean, but it will be better than without tape.

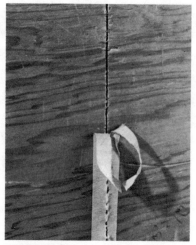

TAPE PEELED away reveals cleaner cut made with this technique.

Crushed threads

A hand-operated thread restorer does the job. It slips over the bolt at a point where good threads remain. Claws are tightened until the cutting edge is inside a groove. You rotate the tool over the damaged part and the cutter restores the threads to let the nut pass.

Where enough threads are exposed, a standard thread-cutting die of the correct size may also be used.